I0520585

BEYOND
RENT CHECKS

A Faith-Based Guide to Purposeful Property

Management

By

Jeannie Armstrong

Copyright © 2025 Jeannie Armstrong

All rights reserved.

ISBN: 979-8-9931561-0-1

Published by Legacy Light Press LLC

No part of this publication may be reproduced, distributed, or transmitted in any form or by any means, including photocopying, recording, or other electronic or mechanical methods, without the prior written permission of the author or publisher, except in the case of brief quotations embodied in critical reviews and certain other noncommercial uses permitted by copyright law.

Dedication

To the One who entrusted me with this message—thank You for the grace to steward it.

To my sons—Joseph, Benjamin, and Kristian—each of you is part of the legacy this book carries.

To my grandchildren—Yasmine, Hannah, Evan, and Maja Jean, may you walk in peace, purpose, and the wisdom of God in every season.

This book is a reflection of love, a testimony of grace, and a prayer for every generation to honor God with their decisions.

TABLE OF CONTENTS

Acknowledgments..6

Preface 8

A Guide to Reading *Beyond Rent Checks*................................11

Introduction 16

Chapter 1: The Foundation: Biblical Principles for Property

Stewardship..21

Chapter 2: Conquering Guilt: Peace in Profitable Stewardship 40

Chapter 3: From Lax to Lawful: Building Unshakable Boundaries 51

Chapter 4: The Gates of Discernment: Mastering Screening's

Foundation..73

Chapter 5: The Practical Blueprint: Steps to Finding Your Ideal

Tenant 83

Chapter 6: The Sacred Agreement: Building a Thorough Lease 111

Chapter 7: Partnering with Professionals: Working with Contractors and Vendors 130

Chapter 8: Managing the Tenancy Life Cycle and Challenges 149

Chapter 9: Cultivating Community: Valuing Your Responsible Tenants 167

Chapter 10: Protecting Your Well-Being: Sustaining Yourself as a Christian Landlord 179

Conclusion 191

Final Encouragement: Keep Stewarding, Keep Growing 195

Acknowledgments

I thank God for the grace to write and the courage to share.

This book was born in quiet moments, hard decisions, and faithful obedience.

To my husband, George—thank you for walking beside me in both life and mission.

To Joseph—your mindset, marketing strategy, writing support, and feedback on key chapters helped shape this message with clarity and conviction.

To Benjamin—your moral encouragement, processing support, and thoughtful engagement with the chapters and title gave me strength and perspective when I needed it most.

To Kasia—thank you for your technical insight, emotional support, and careful reading of various chapters with a discerning eye.

To my church family, my friends, and the women in my Facebook community—thank you for your prayers, encouragement, and spiritual companionship.

May this book serve as a seed of clarity and courage in your own season of sorting and surrender.

Preface

Real estate is magnetic. It draws in dreamers, doers, and those determined to build something lasting. The promise is undeniable: wealth, freedom, legacy. But hidden beneath the glossy headlines and success stories is a sobering truth: what promises the most can also cost the most.

In the vast landscape of entrepreneurship, few ventures hold the promise and peril quite like real estate. It's a field often romanticized, painted with visions of passive income, generational wealth, and boundless freedom. And for good reason. Every wealthy person I know—or have studied—has real estate somewhere in their portfolio. It's not just a trend; it's a pattern. So, is real estate a good investment? Absolutely. And it's always a good time to invest in real estate, if you're prepared. That's why this book exists, not just to inspire you with what's possible, but to equip you with what's practical. Because in real estate, success isn't just about what you acquire, it's about how you steward it.

If you're like me, you stepped into real estate with good intentions, seeking financial freedom, stability for your family, and maybe even a way to bless others. But somewhere along the way, the dream began to feel less like an opportunity and more like a daily grind. You know the late-night phone calls that jolt you awake, bringing with them the familiar dread of urgent repairs or unforeseen crises. The stream of maintenance issues is unending, each one a relentless draw on your time, energy, and financial reserves. Then there are the rent checks that arrive consistently late—or, sometimes, not at all—leaving you with a gnawing anxiety as you navigate your own responsibilities. The delicate balance of addressing lease violations and the potential for legal complications creates a persistent tension, often leaving you to question if you're truly suited for this demanding work.

And beneath these daily struggles, a deeper, more profound question inevitably surfaces, one that speaks to the very heart of your calling: Is it genuinely possible to fulfill your role as a faithful steward in this business without sacrificing your peace? Can faith truly be the bedrock of your decisions, guiding your management of these properties and relationships, when faced with such relentless worldly pressures? This isn't merely about financial success; it's about upholding your values, about stewarding what has been entrusted to you, and finding a way to maintain spiritual equilibrium and inner calm in a profession that often feels anything but peaceful.

The good news? Yes—you can absolutely honor God and still thrive in real estate management. You can trade stress and late-night worries for peace, purpose, and confidence in Him. And yes, your business can be more than contracts and rent checks; it can be part of your calling.

***Beyond Rent Checks* isn't just about managing properties—it's about becoming a faithful steward of what God has placed in your hands.** Inside, you'll find a practical, step-by-step blueprint to confidently handle tenants, leases, repairs, contractors, and policies. You'll learn how to have the hard conversations that protect your business and your boundaries. And you'll confront the inner struggles, guilt, fear, and self-doubt that have held you back from fully embracing both Godly purpose and profit.

More than anything, you'll discover how to move beyond the grind of chasing rent checks and step into a way of working that brings lasting profit, true clarity, and peace that honors God.

Inside these pages, you'll also encounter my signature framework—*Sorting Season*™—a concept born from decades of counseling and property management. It's the moment when accountability shakes the tree and clarity replaces confusion. It's not just a management phase; it's a spiritual shift. And it's one of the most transformative tools I've used to lead with conviction and protect peace.

So, if you're ready to trade stress for strength, confusion for clarity, and frustration for purpose, this book was written for you.

A Guide to Reading *Beyond Rent Checks*

This isn't a book to skim and shelve; it's a journey of faith, stewardship, and transformation. As you move through these pages, you'll not only hear my story but also be invited to reflect, take notes, and put biblical principles into practice.

This is more than just a book; it's an opportunity to experience the divine power of God when you surrender to His purpose for your life. While it begins with my personal journey, it invites you, the reader, to face and overcome the internal barriers that hinder a true Christian mindset.

The book is intentionally interactive. You'll encounter moments to pause and ponder, along with prompts that invite you to ask deeper questions. It's designed to help you grow, transform, and experience the peace that comes from faithfully stewarding the assets God has entrusted to you.

Beyond Rent Checks is deeply rooted in Scripture. You'll find Bible verses woven throughout because I believe everything we encounter as real estate investors has already been addressed by God in His Word. So when we talk about setting boundaries, drafting leases, working with contractors, or navigating tenant relationships, the guidance isn't just my opinion; it's grounded in what God has already said.

To help you get the most out of Beyond Rent Checks, each chapter concludes with a Chapter Reflections and Takeaways:

This section is your moment to pause, process, and prepare. It's where spiritual insight meets practical action, helping you internalize the chapter's message and move forward with clarity and conviction.

Key Truths to Carry Forward

These are the distilled highlights—the spiritual and strategic truths that define the chapter. They remind the reader what matters most and why it matters.

Purpose:

- Reinforce the chapter's core message

- Help readers remember what to hold onto when challenges arise

- Offer spiritual clarity in the midst of practical complexity

Examples:

- Boundaries are not barriers; they're bridges to peace.

- Clarity is kindness, especially in conflict.

- Stewardship is not just about property; it's about people.

Action Steps to Apply

This is where insight becomes movement. These steps invite the reader to take what they've learned and do something with it—whether it's a small shift or a bold decision.

Purpose:

- Translate spiritual and strategic lessons into real-world action

- Encourage momentum, even if imperfect

- Provide tangible next steps for growth

Examples:

- Review your lease agreement and highlight any areas that need clearer language.

- Schedule a monthly property walkthrough to stay proactive.

- Write down one boundary you've been avoiding and commit to enforcing it with grace.

Prayer:

A short, heartfelt prayer to help the reader invite God into their stewardship journey. It's not just a spiritual pause; it's a reminder that they're not managing alone.

Purpose:

- Anchor the reader's heart in God's presence

- Offer comfort, courage, and spiritual alignment

- Reinforce that stewardship is a calling, not a burden

Example:

Lord, give me wisdom to lead with clarity, grace to enforce with peace, and strength to steward well what You've placed in my hands. Amen.

Scriptures to Meditate On

These verses deepen the chapter's message and offer spiritual grounding. Each one should be paired with a brief, practical reflection to help the reader connect the Word to their work.

Purpose:

- Provide biblical support for the chapter's themes

- Encourage spiritual reflection and personal growth

- Help readers see their role through the lens of Scripture

Example:

> **Proverbs 27:23** – *"Be diligent to know the state of your flocks..."* Stay attentive to your properties and tenants. Stewardship begins with awareness.

This book is meant to be read slowly and prayerfully. Share it with other landlords, real estate investors, pastors, ministry leaders, or Christian entrepreneurs—anyone who desires to faithfully steward the gifts God has entrusted to them.

Introduction

Why I Got into Real Estate Investment (and Why You Need This Guide)

W hen people ask how I got started in real estate, I usually give them the clean version: "I bought a single-family home, rented it out, then bought another."

It sounds simple. Safe. Strategic.

But the real story, the one that actually shaped me, is far more complicated.

I didn't step into real estate as a bold entrepreneur with a vision board and a five-year plan. I stepped in cautiously. Fearfully. With shaky confidence and what felt like mustard-seed faith.

At the time, I thought I was just trying to build a little financial security, a small portfolio.

What I didn't know was that real estate investing would become something much deeper: a platform where God would confront my fears, rebuild my trust, and grow me into a faithful steward.

Long before I ever held the keys to a rental home, I was playing life safe. I followed the rules, worked hard, and did everything in my power to protect my sons. I overthought every decision, trying to anticipate every possible outcome. I had convinced myself that if I planned enough, prepared enough, and perfected everything, I could avoid pain—not just for me, but for everyone I loved.

What I didn't understand back then was that all of that over-functioning—the perfectionism, the control, the anxiety—was rooted in trauma. I had trusted God before, and in my mind, it hadn't worked out well. Somewhere deep inside, I had decided that I needed to be my own safety net. I still loved God, but I was also quietly angry with Him. The irony was that I desperately wanted to trust God. I even took decisive steps toward Him, but I never deceived myself; I never truly surrendered. I trusted Him with eternity, but I lived in fear of His control of my tomorrow. And definitely not with my today.

Ironically, I was working as a therapist, specializing in treating anxiety. I knew all about the cycle: fear, avoidance, control. I understood that healing meant exposure to the thing you feared most. And I preached it to others. But when it came to my own journey, I was still holding on tightly. Still stuck in the loop.

Then came the nudge, the unmistakable conviction from God that it was time to move. Not just physically, but spiritually. To walk forward. To trust again. To take a risk with Him.

So I did. I felt like I didn't have a choice. I wanted Him, and He wanted me.

Real estate became my classroom of faith. Every property, every lease, every interaction with a tenant became a place of refinement. I was stretched, challenged, and humbled. I made mistakes. I wanted to quit. But I kept walking, and God kept meeting me. Not with immediate success or smooth sailing, but with growth. Clarity. Peace. Power.

I now understand that what I was doing wasn't just investing, I was learning to steward. And faithful stewardship, especially for the Christian landlord, is about more than good paperwork and rent collection. It's about living and managing from a place of trust and order. It's about letting go of control, embracing biblical boundaries, and building something that reflects God's character, not just our own ambition.

There were many times when I wanted to throw in the towel, like when interest rates rose and mortgage payments ballooned, or when repairs I couldn't afford came in waves. But each time, I prayed and chose to keep going. Yes, I kept going because I needed to trust Him. Not because it was easy, but because I had to step out on His promises. I had to believe He would be faithful, that He would meet me at every turn, and that obedience—even in uncertainty—would lead me where I needed to go. *Beyond Rent Checks* is the result of that movement.

Let me be clear about what this book is—and what it isn't.

This is not a book about scaling a portfolio or aggressive real estate leverage.

However, as a result of this book, many landlords will grow into owning many, many properties, but that's not the heartbeat of this work. The heartbeat is stewarding well what God has already placed in your hands.

Before expansion ever becomes a possibility, faithfulness, structure, and covenant-minded care must come first. That is the work we are doing here—building the kind of foundation God can trust with more.

This book is for the Christian who feels called to real estate but wants to honor God every step of the way.

It's for the landlord who's trying to run a business with integrity, but sometimes feels overwhelmed, uncertain, or out of alignment.

It's for the one who's done the budgeting, the saving, the studying, and still feels stuck or unsure of what to do next.

It's for the person who keeps questioning if they're really cut out for this, or if they've missed the mark somehow.

And it's for Christian entrepreneurs, landlords, pastors, and ministry leaders who want their work to reflect their faith, serve others, and build lasting impact—without burning out or compromising their values.

If that's you, this book is your blueprint.

A path toward peace in your process, profit with purpose, and clarity about why this calling matters, to you and to God.

Here, you'll find a Christian landlord's blueprint—not just for business, but for spiritual formation through business. You'll learn how to build leases with wisdom, manage tenants with grace and authority, build win/win relationships with contractors, and structure your property management in ways that protect your peace and reflect God's order.

But more than anything, I pray you'll be reminded that your story—like mine—is God's. He can use your obedience to bless others. That even the scariest steps can lead to the deepest transformation.

Let's begin, not with fear, but with faith.

Chapter 1: The Foundation: Biblical Principles for Property Stewardship

Called Without A Map

My real estate journey began in a way that felt both terrifying and divine. I had no roadmap, no mentor holding my hand. Just research, prayer, and a deep inner sense that God was calling me to move. It wasn't just the fear of a bad investment; it was the deeper, more insidious fear that God might not come through, a whisper from past disappointments that echoed louder than any financial projection. Yet, amidst the swirling anxieties, a quiet conviction settled within me – not a booming voice from heaven, but a deep, unshakeable peace that defied all logical reasons for doubt. It was a surprising calm, a sense of rightness in my spirit, that affirmed this path was indeed divinely appointed, even if the roadmap was still a blur.

Favor in the First Step

I remember the day I got the keys to my first property, a moment that felt heavy with responsibility, yet filled with a surprising surge of hope. It was a small, three-bedroom, one-bath home in a B– or C+ neighborhood, priced at $48,000. The elderly couple who owned it were eager to relocate closer to their adult children in North Carolina, and their urgency, thankfully, became our opportunity.

I walked through its quiet, empty rooms, heart pounding, and thought, Lord, what are we doing? A whisper of desperation, yet tinged with a nascent hope. But as I took it all in, a wave of satisfaction washed over me. The house, though modest in price, felt like a true gem: move-in ready with pretty hardwood flooring that gleamed under fresh paint. It was a charming combo of old and new, and I particularly loved the black antique rotary phone still mounted on the wall – I even imagined my future tenants enjoying the unique conversation piece it would spark. Stepping into the expansive yard, I envisioned life happening there. A concrete-covered patio with an outdoor ceiling fan invited quiet evenings and bustling family cookouts. I felt genuinely good about the physical environment, knowing it was a place someone could truly call home. And finding such a property for $48,000? That felt like nothing short of divine favor.

This wasn't just about money. It wasn't even just about opportunity. For me, this was about obedience—about reclaiming trust in a God I still sometimes feared "didn't play fair". I was stepping into a new chapter, not with full confidence, but with what became a surrendered heart. I'd spent months preparing—reading books, watching videos, studying markets. I kept stalling, questioning if I was ready. I knew that all this was just fear in disguise. Faith, I knew, required action.

The time had come to dive my whole body in. I had spent way too long dipping a toe in the water, playing it safe. I always managed to keep a safety net. But, as I said, it was time, and I didn't have a choice. Not because I was backed into a corner by circumstance, but because I was convicted by truth.

I had reached a point where the tension between what I knew and what I was living became unbearable. I couldn't keep pretending I was stewarding well when I was really just surviving. I couldn't keep calling it grace when it was really avoidance. I couldn't keep asking God to bless what I hadn't built with Him.

It was that place where you know—deep down—you haven't fully surrendered. Not because you don't love God. Not because you don't believe in Him. But because the last time you trusted Him, it didn't work out the way you hoped.

You obeyed. You prayed. You stepped out in faith. And instead of a breakthrough, you got brokenness. Instead of favor, you got fallout. Instead of peace, you got pain.

So now, when He asks for another yes, your heart flinches. You hesitate—not out of rebellion, but out of self-protection. You're not resisting God. You're just trying to survive the disappointment.

But here's the truth I had to face: Delayed obedience is still disobedience. And fear of the outcome is not a reason to ignore the instruction.

I had to confront the fact that I was holding back—not because I didn't trust God's power, but because I doubted His plan for me. I was still carrying the weight of what didn't work before. Still nursing the wounds of obedience that didn't lead to the result I wanted.

But God doesn't promise us outcomes. He promises us presence. And sometimes, peace doesn't come from the result; it comes from the surrender.

So yes, I said I didn't have a choice. Because I had reached the end of my own logic, my own strategy, my own strength. And in that place— where my control ran out—obedience became the only door left.

And when I walked through it, even trembling, even unsure, I found Him waiting. Not with explanations, but with peace. Not with guarantees, but with grace. Not with everything I wanted, but with everything I needed.

Because God doesn't call the equipped, He equips the surrendered.

The Blessing and the Blind Spot

Soon after advertising the property, a young professional couple moved in. They were a dream: paying their rent not just on time, but often early, taking beautiful care of the home, and hardly ever requesting repairs. This is the favor of God. This is how it's supposed to go. I exhaled, the tension I hadn't realized I was holding finally released. Man, this is easy.

Encouraged by this success, I quickly purchased a second property. This one was a significant step up: twice the size, a three-bedroom, three-full-bathroom home with ample living space, including a large living room, a family room with a fireplace, an eat-in kitchen, and a separate dining room. Moderately priced at $65,000 in a nice B neighborhood, this was a VA foreclosure that demanded major renovations; my first true encounter with contractors. I soon learned that not all contractors are created equally, nor do they always possess the advertised skill set. Since I was already committed to doing a significant portion of the work myself: painting several rooms, pulling up old carpet, refinishing hardwood flooring, and even reglazing tubs and sinks, I found myself at the property nearly every day. While the larger tasks like fortified roofing, appliance installation, electrical work, or fencing were beyond my capabilities, my consistent presence and persistent questioning, though initially focused on my own tasks, inevitably led to an unexpected level of oversight. I'm convinced this direct involvement ensured I got my money's worth from the contractors, saving significant time and expense. Despite the inherent challenges—given my limited knowledge then about comprehensive renovations, drafting clear contracts, and adhering to a realistic budget within a 10% margin—the project, in hindsight, progressed well. With the renovation complete and the property gleaming, I felt a fresh wave of optimism. This time, I was even more prepared, eager for the next chapter of responsible stewardship to begin.

When Stewardship Gets Messy

And for a while, that second home seemed to follow the same rhythm: responsible tenants, timely payments, and minimal drama. I breathed easy. These tenants were two long-term city workers, and on paper, it felt like a win. But looking back, a red flag had already started waving.

Their previous landlord didn't call me directly. Instead, his real estate agent reached out—not to offer a factual reference, but to campaign for their tenancy. He told me they needed to move quickly because the property was being sold. He painted them as ideal tenants, glossing over the truth with a brush dipped in urgency and charm. I didn't ask enough questions. I didn't dig deeper. I was still riding the high of early success, and their pleas to rent my freshly renovated house tugged at my heart more than their credit scores tugged at my discernment.

I ignored the numbers. I ignored the nudge in my spirit. I convinced myself that I had found a formula for passive income and peace. After all, they were nice people with a sister who was a doctor who offered to co-sign. Well, needless to say, I reasoned they were full-grown adults with two city jobs between them, so surely I would not have a problem with the rent or tenancy. Things went well for the first several months until things began to shift.

The irony is, everything I had experienced up to that point had been real. The joy, the purpose, the sense of calling; it was all true. But it was only one side of the coin. The other side was about to rear its ugly head, teaching me that there is no such thing as a one-sided coin!

The household dynamic felt unstable. There always seemed to be more people visiting than on the lease. Noise complaints started trickling in. Neighbors who once waved now call with concerns. Abandoned vehicles began to appear in the yard like warning signs I didn't want to read. I felt the tension building, like a storm gathering overhead, but I didn't know how to respond.

Inside, I was torn. My internal dialogue became a tug-of-war:

They're paying the rent. Should I really interfere? People have the right to live their own way, in their own place. I'm a Christian. I should be gracious, patient, and understanding… right?

But the truth was, I wasn't being gracious; I was being afraid.

I was scared to have hard conversations. Scared to confront behavior that didn't align with the standards I had set. Scared to be labeled the "bad guy." I wanted to be liked. I wanted to be seen as kind, flexible, and easygoing. I wanted to be a "good landlord."

But in that desire to be liked, I abandoned something far more important: the authority God had entrusted to me.

I was called to steward, not to shrink. But I shrank.

Instead of leading, I reacted. Instead of setting the tone, I absorbed the chaos. I became a landlord who chased rent checks and danced around dysfunction. I kept fixing things: leaky faucets, broken fences, busted windows, but I wasn't fixing the root. I had no system. No structure. No clarity. Just a growing list of repairs and a gnawing sense that I was losing control.

And the truth is, I wasn't just losing control of the property; I was losing control of my peace, my purpose, and my posture as a leader.

> **Pause and consider:** When in your stewardship journey have you been hesitant to act—not because you didn't care, but because fear or uncertainty held you back?

Eventually, they left quietly, in the middle of the night, under the cover of darkness—leaving behind a mess. Financial. Emotional. Spiritual.

That moment forced me to reflect; it absolutely began my turning point. I was angry with these tenants, but angrier with myself. Why had I just let this happen? Why was I scared to go to my property, and so on? Yes, I was compassionate, maybe even graceful, but I wasn't prudent. I was definitely not operating as a steward of my gift.

Recognizing my missteps made one thing clear: I needed to see exactly where my systems had failed—but the truth was, I didn't have a system. When I checked my lease, the gaps were glaring—clauses missing that should have protected my interests. A quick calculation of what it would cost to re-rent the property made it painfully clear: my profits had quietly walked out with the tenants, under the cover of darkness.

The financial hit stung, but it was only part of the story. I began grappling with a deeper question: how much was I truly willing to pay to do this right? Landlording, I was discovering, was far messier than I'd imagined. I didn't yet have the answer to what I was willing to pay, only what I would not: my peace of mind, my relationship with God, sacrificing people for profits, or compromising my own integrity.

In contemplating these costs—both the visible and invisible—I was reminded of an encounter several years earlier, long before I even purchased my first rental property.

My husband and I had spent a full day riding around Mobile with a woman who, by her count, owned 106 rental properties. She had wanted to sell a few of them to get us started. It was a no-nonsense deal, saving time, money, and avoiding all the usual red tape. I valued the clarity and trust, especially when she said, "Pay me what you think is fair. No banks, no haggling, just a fair price." Owner financing, no strings attached.

We toured several of her rentals, some still tenant-occupied. A few had holes in the floors. To be honest, there wasn't a single property I would have felt comfortable renting to anyone. Some looked abandoned, but people were living in them nonetheless.

My husband casually asked her, "Are you a slumlord?"

Her reply was blunt. "I sure am. I keep the rent so low, they can't find a cheaper place, so they never leave."

We saw children sleeping beside exposed wires and families settling into conditions they likely felt they had no choice but to accept. And the justification? I'm sure you've heard it too, more times than I care to admit—from contractors, landlords, even real estate agents: "You don't have to live here."

That moment had seared itself into my heart. I knew I didn't want to be harsh or greedy, but I also couldn't afford to keep operating without discernment or structure. I wanted to steward these properties with integrity and caring for people without sacrificing my calling or my conscience.

> **Take a moment:** How do you want to be remembered in your role as a **steward**?
>
> What values or convictions shape the way you handle property, people, and problems;

This is why I chose my book title: Beyond Rent Checks. Because property management is about much more than just collecting money or rent checks, it's about stewarding lives, homes, and communities. It's about balance, not becoming a slumlord who neglects responsibility, or a guilt-ridden landlord who avoids necessary boundaries. Instead, it's about stewarding with peace, purpose, and yes, profit.

Stewardship Starts with Structure

The Bible says, "Let all things be done decently and in order" (1 Corinthians 14:40). That verse isn't just about worship services—it applies to how we manage everything: our property, how we treat people, and how we run our business.

I began to realize that order isn't in opposition to grace; it's what makes grace sustainable. Without structure, our compassion becomes chaos. Without boundaries, our kindness becomes enabling.

From that point on, I made some changes. I started reading my Bible with fresh eyes, seeking what it said about boundaries, order, and the meaning of justice—and I found guidance at every turn. The more I studied, the more I saw that real stewardship requires structure, a system of order. It's more than paperwork; it's a framework for peace and order. And no matter where I looked, whether at people, processes, or priorities, it kept bringing me back to one place: *the lease.*

31

The Lease: A Tool for Peace

At first glance, a lease might seem like just paperwork—a formality to get signed and filed. But I've come to see it as something far deeper. The lease is one of the most powerful tools a landlord has, not just for legal protection, but for spiritual and emotional peace.

It's a tool for stewardship. A tool for ministry. A tool for clarity. And ultimately, a tool for peace.

When I Restructured Everything

I went back and restructured my lease completely. This wasn't about piling on rules for the sake of control—it was about creating clarity, boundaries, and a framework that honored both my tenants and my responsibilities as a steward.

I made sure it included:

- Clear rent due dates and late fees

- Online-only payment policies

- Guidelines around maintenance responsibilities

- A clear guest and occupancy policy

- Noise and parking rules

- Pet requirements

- Default and abandonment clauses

Each element served a purpose. They weren't punitive—they were practical expressions of care and order. Clarity is kindness. Structure is love in action. By reshaping the lease this way, I wasn't just protecting my property; I was creating a system where everyone knew what to expect, accountability was clear, and peace could exist—for me and for my tenants.

Unpacking What a Covenant-Based Lease Looks Like

After making these changes, I began to see the lease differently—not just as rules on paper, but as a covenant.

A covenant-based lease is rooted in mutual respect, accountability, and responsibility. It's not only about what tenants must do; it's about what I, as a landlord, commit to as well.

While due dates, fees, and pet policies are essential, a covenant-based lease communicates a deeper principle: we are in this arrangement with integrity, fairness, and intentionality. It establishes boundaries that honor both parties and sets the tone for every interaction.

Where my previous lease was reactive, focusing on problems after they arose, this covenant-based approach is proactive. It anticipates challenges, fosters trust, and creates a framework where both tenant and landlord know what to expect and how to engage with one another respectfully.

It's not just business, it's a relationship. And relationships thrive in clarity.

Grace, Boundaries, and Ministry

As I embraced this structure, I also realized that property management isn't just a business; it's a ministry.

Grace and boundaries aren't contradictory; they're complementary. Jesus was tender and sharp, forgiving yet holding accountable. As Christian landlords, we are called to the same balance: operate with compassion, but also with courage.

Love means holding people to their commitments. Grace doesn't mean silence. Forgiveness doesn't mean enabling.

My role isn't to fix my tenants. My role is to faithfully steward what God has given me—with love, yes, but also with structure. I serve a faithful God—one who meets me every time I choose to trust Him. One of my most sacred sayings is:

"God will meet you in a place called obedience."

And that obedience includes how I manage what He's entrusted to me. The lease is part of that obedience. It's a reflection of order, accountability, and care.

What Comes Next

In the chapters ahead, we'll get practical. I'll walk you through real scenarios and the systems I use: leases, notices, screening, and maintenance.

In all we do, we hold to a simple philosophy:

We serve with compassion and wisdom, using systems that reflect God's order.

This is what true stewardship looks like. And it begins with a yes. Even when that yes feels scary, risky, overwhelming, or uncertain—we say yes.

Because God doesn't call the equipped; He equips the called. That's where stewardship and obedience meet.

Chapter 1 Reflections and Takeaways: The Foundation—Biblical Principles for Property Stewardship

Key Truths to Carry Forward

- **Stewardship begins with obedience, not perfection**. We say yes to God's way of doing business, even when we don't see it ourselves. My journey started with a leap of faith, not a fully formed plan.

- **Fear cannot lead.** Structure, clarity, and courage are part of faithful stewardship. My initial fear led to inaction, which ultimately created more chaos and loss. Learning to trust God meant acting in courage, even when I felt uncertain.

- **Stewardship means holding space for both compassion and boundaries.** They are not in conflict or mutually exclusive. My desire for grace without clear rules only led to escalating problems, ultimately hurting everyone involved.

- **Property management can be a ministry, even if no one else notices**. God does. Operating faithfully in the marketplace, providing safe and decent housing, and creating stable communities are all forms of ministry.

- **Faithful stewardship blesses both landlord and tenant**. When we honor God, we create stability and dignity for others. A well-structured system benefits everyone involved.

- **Small, consistent steps matter more than dramatic leaps**. Steady faithfulness builds long-term fruit. My daily presence at the second property, though focused on tasks, taught me the power of consistent involvement.

Action Steps to Apply

1. Reflect on whether fear or uncertainty has stopped you from taking action. Pray for courage to move forward in obedience. Identify one specific instance or area in your life where fear has held you back in stewardship.

2. Commit to viewing property management as stewardship and ministry, not just business. Consider how your approach can bring stability and dignity to others.

3. Choose one small, consistent habit you can practice this week (such as a prayer before reviewing applications, a daily ten-minute property walk, or simply organizing your digital files) to reinforce faithfulness in the "little things."

4. What systems do you currently have in place, and are they helping you reflect God's order, or are they making it harder to steward well? Focus on one specific system (e.g., how you

handle maintenance requests or tenant screening) and assess its effectiveness.

Prayer of Thankfulness

Lord, thank You for entrusting me with the resources and responsibilities You've placed in my hands. Give me the wisdom to steward them well, the courage to act when fear tempts me to shrink back, and the grace to balance compassion with healthy boundaries. May my work reflect Your order, bring peace to my household and tenants, and glorify You in every detail. In Jesus's name, amen.

Scriptures to Meditate On

- **Leviticus 25:23** *'The land must not be sold permanently, because the land is mine and you reside in my land as foreigners and strangers."* Your role is not owner, but steward. Recognizing that the land belongs to God shifts your mindset from possession to purpose.

- **Proverbs 16:3** *"Commit to the Lord whatever you do, and he will establish your plans."* When you surrender your property decisions to God, He brings clarity, direction, and peace to your stewardship.

- **Matthew 6:33** *"But seek first his kingdom and his righteousness, and all these things will be given to you as well."* Stewardship begins with seeking God's priorities. When you manage property with integrity and kingdom values, provision follows.

- **Psalm 37:5** *"Commit your way to the Lord; trust in him and he will do this."* Entrusting your property management to God allows you to release control and rest in His timing and provision.

Chapter 2: Conquering Guilt: Peace in Profitable Stewardship

A s Christian landlords, we often find ourselves wrestling with an unexpected internal conflict: an unspoken, moral, or spiritual discomfort tied to reconciling faith, profit, and the practicalities of property stewardship. This conflict takes shape as guilt—not the guilt of criminality or overt sin, but a deeper, more insidious self-reproach that slowly erodes the joy and clarity we once had.

It begins subtly, like a whisper of uncertainty:

Am I doing the right thing?

Am I truly honoring God through this business?

Is this calling even holy?

That whisper becomes a persistent undercurrent, robbing us of peace, disturbing our confidence, and casting shadows over every decision. Soon, even routine tasks like collecting rent, enforcing leases, or evicting problematic tenants become emotionally fraught. What should be stewardship begins to feel like selfishness. The blessing of business turns into a burden of doubt.

This chapter peels back the layers of that struggle. We'll examine the roots of that guilt, confront it with biblical truth, and provide a framework to help you shed it while embracing peace and profitable stewardship

We'll examine the roots of that guilt, confront it with biblical truth, and provide a framework to help you shed it while embracing peace and profitable stewardship.

Before we dive in, let's pause and reflect on a few hard, heart-checking questions:

1. Have you ever hesitated to enforce a lease out of fear of being "un-Christian"?

2. Have you felt uneasy about making a profit, even when your costs and risks were high?

3. Do you struggle to balance mercy and accountability, especially with tenants going through hardship?

4. Have you felt burned out from helping people who don't seem to respect your generosity?

5. Have you ever hesitated to enforce a lease out of fear of being "un-Christian"?

6. Have you felt uneasy about making a profit, even when your costs and risks were

If so, you're not alone—and you're not off track. You're human. And more importantly, you're a steward. The good news is that this chapter was written for you. Together, we will walk through the pain, the truth, and the release together.

When Idealism Meets Reality

Like many others, I entered the world of rental property with idealism. I believed that I could be different—that I could reflect Christ in every transaction and interaction. Coming from a social work background, compassion came naturally. I was used to advocating, supporting, and listening. My heart was wide open, and I believed that faith, grace, and business could seamlessly align.

But the real world brought friction.

Rent came late. Promises were broken. Systems failed. Tenants took advantage of kindness. Contractors misrepresented the facts. County departments dragged their feet. Slowly, my trust began to erode—not just in others, but in myself and my ability to steward well.

Then life delivered a blow that cut even deeper: my son was incarcerated.

Suddenly, the weight I carried extended beyond my business. As a mother, a believer, and a business owner, I was forced to confront a harsh question: Had my trust—too freely given—failed both my family and my calling?

The guilt compounded: professional, emotional, and spiritual. I tried to compartmentalize, to keep my roles separate. But guilt doesn't stay in neat boxes. It spills over. It affects how you show up in meetings, how you communicate with tenants, and how you make decisions. It saps your joy and confidence until everything feels cloudy and heavy

All of This Revealed a Painful Truth

All of this revealed a painful truth: I had been trying to run a business on empathy alone.

I saw people's struggles and felt responsible for fixing them. When tenants were behind, I'd pay their utilities out of pocket or extend deadlines long past reason. I told myself it was grace, but in reality, it was guilt wearing a halo.

I carried burdens that weren't mine to carry. I thought I had to absorb every hardship, every excuse, every shortfall, believing it was the only way to honor God. But Scripture reminds us there's a balance. Galatians 6:2 says, *"Bear one another's burdens,"* **yet verse 5 warns,** *"For each will have to bear his own load."*

I had blurred the lines, taking on responsibilities that weren't mine— and in the process, my own stewardship suffered.

One day, my husband—also my business partner—looked me in the eye and asked, "Are you a therapist or a business owner?"

His question hit hard. Not because it was harsh, but because it was true. I had allowed guilt—not God—to guide my decisions. I was carrying burdens that weren't mine, letting misplaced compassion overshadow wise stewardship.

That realization was a turning point. True stewardship isn't about martyrdom; it's about discernment. It's about knowing when to help and when to allow others to manage the weight God has given them. Only then could I act faithfully, honor God, and find peace in my work.

The Trap of Misplaced Compassion

One tenant stands out in particular—a single mother, recently unemployed, behind on rent. Her story broke my heart. Every fiber of my social-worker self wanted to help. And I did—again and again.

But as months passed and excuses piled up, I began to dread opening her emails. I felt manipulated, emotionally drained, and financially strapped. Still, I hesitated to take action.

Why?

Because even though I never said it aloud, I was *living out* the lie that profit and compassion were mutually exclusive. That to honor God, I had to absorb the burden myself. That to be merciful, I had to be silent and sacrificial—even when it hurt.

But mercy without boundaries is not mercy—it's confusion. Compassion without accountability creates chaos. I was trying to save people when God called me to steward.

That's when the Holy Spirit reminded me: grace and boundaries can coexist. They must. One without the other isn't stewardship, it's imbalance.

Reframing the Calling: From Ownership to Stewardship

Psalm 24:1 tells us, *"The earth is the Lord's, and everything in it, the world, and all who live in it."*
This means we don't own anything. Not the properties. Not the people. Not even the outcomes.

We are stewards. And stewardship is not weakness; it's responsibility.

Jesus praised stewards who multiplied their resources, who took risks, and who managed wisely and without fear (Matthew 25:14-30). He never condemned profitability—but He did confront laziness, fear, and false humility.

This truth changed everything for me.
I am not a savior. I am not a bank. I am not a martyr.
I am a steward of what God placed in my hands.

And stewardship includes:

- Setting healthy boundaries from a Christian perspective

- Charging fair rent

- Requiring accountability

- Pursuing sustainability over sentimentality

Yes, that last one was huge for me. I would rent to a cute little baby who didn't have a job and overlook that Daddy had been looking for one for years! Guess who ended up paying the rent?

When we operate this way, profit isn't selfish; it's fruit.And fruit is meant to be harvested, multiplied, and shared—not left to rot on the vine out of guilt or misplaced compassion.

From Guilt to Growth: What God Actually Expects

Get really clear on this: **that gnawing guilt and confusion about how to steward your properties are not from God.** He is not the author of confusion. Guilt that shames, paralyzes, or discourages is not the Holy Spirit. God convicts us to correct, restore, and strengthen; not to crush us or weigh us down with condemnation or confusion.

Sometimes what we label as "conviction" is actually emotional or mental exhaustion, a signal that we've carried too much for too long. When your mind and heart are depleted, even good discernment can feel heavy. Recognizing that difference allows you to rest, realign, and respond from wisdom instead of weariness.

Here's a simple reflective exercise—rooted in both Scripture and sound psychology—to help you shift from guilt or mental paralysis to peace and clarity.

Closing Encouragement: Peace Is a Byproduct of Obedience

This journey isn't about choosing between faith and finances; it's about aligning both under God's design. You don't need to operate as if they're in opposition.

Your business is not a distraction from your calling; it *is* your calling. And God is not honored by your burnout; He's honored by your boundaries.
He's not glorified in your guilt; He's glorified in your growth.

Let go—by His strength—of anything that holds you back from walking in your true purpose. As landlords, your purpose is to steward what's been placed in your hands as gifts from God.

Take hold of your stewardship and step forward—not with hesitation, but with peace.

There is profit in purpose. And there is peace when it's rooted in God.

Chapter 2 Reflections and Takeaways: Conquering the Guilt—Finding Peace in Profitable Purposes

Key Truths to Carry Forward

- **Guilt is not your guide; God is.** Guilt pushes you to overextend, overcompensate, and override your peace. But God leads with clarity and conviction, not shame. His voice brings correction, not condemnation. When guilt tries to steer your decisions, pause and ask: *Is this God, or fear talking?*

- **Stewardship requires both compassion and clarity.** Compassion without clarity leads to chaos. Clarity without compassion leads to control. True stewardship lives in the tension of both grace and grit, kindness and boundaries. You're not just managing property; you're modeling kingdom principles.

- **Profit is not the enemy of faith. It can be a fruit of obedience.** Profit isn't greed, it's fruit. When your systems reflect God's order and your decisions reflect His wisdom, increase can follow. Don't shrink from success. God delights in faithful stewardship that multiplies.

- **Healthy boundaries are a form of love: toward yourself, your tenants, and your God.** Boundaries protect your peace, your purpose, and your people. They say, *"I love you enough to be clear."* They also say, *"I love myself enough to be whole."* And most importantly, *"I honor God enough to protect what He's entrusted to me."*

Action Steps to Apply

1. Prayerfully name one area of guilt. What situation keeps replaying in your mind? Write it down. Then release it in prayer.

2. Replace the lie with truth. Find a Scripture that speaks directly to the lie you're believing. Write it somewhere visible this week.

3. Set one stewardship boundary. Choose one business boundary to clarify or reinforce: rent collection, communication cutoff times, or support limits.

4. Invite God into one decision. Whether it's a tough eviction or rent increase, pause and pray before acting. Let peace—not pressure—lead.

Prayer of Release

Father God, thank You for trusting me with this business and these people. I confess the guilt I've carried—some justified, some misplaced—and I surrender it to You. Help me lead with grace and truth. Teach me to steward what You've given without shame, fear, or false humility. I trade the weight of guilt for the wisdom of Your Word. I choose peace. In Jesus's name, amen.

Scriptures to Meditate On

- **Romans 8:1** *'There is now no condemnation for those who are in Christ Jesus."* Condemnation can show up as a mindset rooted in past trauma, causing you to shrink from walking into your calling. This verse reminds you that you are not disqualified from receiving a blessing. You can pursue profitable stewardship with peace, knowing that guilt has no authority over a life anchored in grace.

- **Psalm 24:1** *'The earth is the Lord's, and everything in it."* Your properties belong to God. You are entrusted by Him to steward them. When you manage according to His principles, you can release guilt and rest—knowing the outcome is His to decide, not yours to carry.

- **Matthew 25:21** *'Well done, good and faithful servant... You have been faithful with a few things; I will put you in charge of many things."* Faithfully managing your rental business—honoring leases, maintaining properties, and treating tenants fairly—is kingdom work. When you steward well, even in small things, you position yourself for greater impact and deeper trust from God.

Chapter 3: From Lax to Lawful: Building Unshakable Boundaries

Many Christian landlords struggle with setting firm boundaries. We confuse grace with leniency, mercy with passivity. But God is a God of order (1 Corinthians 14:33), and part of our role as landlords is to maintain order—not just in our units, but in how we conduct ourselves as stewards.

Without clear boundaries, your peace will suffer, your tenants will be confused, and your business will slowly unravel. But with lawful, loving limits in place, you'll experience a renewed sense of confidence, fairness, and peace in your calling.

This chapter turns the corner from structure on paper to structure in practice, because what we tolerate teaches others how to treat our stewardship.

The Cost of Being "Too Nice"

At some point, most Christian landlords face the emotional tug-of-war between compassion and responsibility. Perhaps you've found yourself:

- Letting rent slide repeatedly without consequence.

- Accepting late payments without enforcing fees.

- Feeling awkward about issuing notices or confronting tenant behavior.

- Avoiding tough conversations because you didn't want to seem unkind or "un-Christian."

- Covering costs or making exceptions out of guilt rather than principle.

- Hesitating to enforce rules because you fear being perceived as harsh.

- Sacrificing your own peace of mind to accommodate a tenant's hardship.

These tendencies often come from a sincere place. We don't want to appear greedy. We want to help. We want to show grace. But unstructured grace has a hidden danger: it can quietly morph into enablement. When we let rules slide, avoid difficult conversations, or excuse behavior in the name of kindness, confusion, resentment, and instability begin to take root.

And your sense of calling can quickly become heavy with frustration, guilt, and exhaustion. Research on small business and property management consistently shows that leaders who avoid setting clear boundaries experience higher stress, emotional fatigue, and decision paralysis. Many Christian landlords I've met eventually step away—not because they lack faith, but because the weight of unaddressed conflicts, repeated tenant issues, and blurred personal boundaries becomes overwhelming. Over time, the stress compounds, eroding confidence, diminishing joy, and distorting the very sense of calling that once inspired you to serve.

Here's what I've learned firsthand:

- Lax landlords breed chaos.

- Grace without structure creates resentment.

- Peace cannot survive where there is no order.

- Unenforced rules invite repeated delinquencies.

- Ignoring policies undermines authority and tenant understanding.

- Avoiding difficult conversations delays resolution and increases stress.

- Sacrificing your boundaries for short-term comfort erodes long-term stability, leading to burnout—and in some cases, giving up altogether.

Let me share a real-life example that tested my boundaries and forced me to grow.

A tenant recently submitted only partial rent—$1,000 of the $1,300 due—on the first of the month. This wasn't a mistake or oversight. I suspected it was a protest. The tenant had been dealing with a repair issue in the unit, and while we had been diligent and communicative, I sensed that their frustration was now manifesting through withheld rent.

Importantly, we were still actively working on the repair. Licensed professionals were handling the major components, and we were even considering allowing the tenant to complete a minor portion of the work that didn't require a license. However, that arrangement was still being finalized and had no bearing on their rent obligation.

On the fifth of the month, when the grace period ended and the rent was still not paid in full, I knew it was time to respond. I drafted and sent a formal notice, making sure it addressed all the key points necessary to communicate clearly and maintain accountability:

- The outstanding balance owed.

- The date on which late fees were now being assessed.

- The continued requirement to comply with the lease terms.

The letter was firm, professional, and respectful. I acknowledged their concerns regarding the repair, reassured them of our diligence, and reminded them that rent was a separate, ongoing obligation under our lease agreement.

It wasn't personal. It wasn't emotional. It was the result of having lawful, loving boundaries in place and being willing to stand on them. You'll find a version of this letter included in the digital templates in the bundle, a practical tool designed to help Christian landlords respond professionally and respectfully. We'll explore more of these templates in Chapter 8, showing how they can support every step of property management.

The Biblical Call to Boundaries

Scripture is not silent on boundaries; in fact, they are essential. Creation itself was an act of boundary-setting: God separated light from darkness, land from sea (Genesis 1).

The Garden of Eden had a boundary: One tree was off-limits, teaching us that even paradise requires limits (Genesis 2:17).

Jesus set boundaries: He withdrew from crowds, said "no" to certain requests, and upheld standards even in the face of criticism (Luke 5:16; John 6:66–67).

Boundaries aren't unloving; they're foundational to lasting relationships and orderly communities.

In real estate, this looks like you:

- Enforce your lease terms consistently.

- Charge late fees when rent is late.

- Serve notices when violations occur.

- Say "no" to tenant requests that cannot or should not be accommodated.

Putting Boundaries into Practice

These examples illustrate the principle, but what does it mean in practice? Setting and enforcing boundaries isn't about being harsh or unkind; it's about establishing clear expectations and mutual respect. It's about respect for your tenants, respect for the lease agreements you've both committed to, and respect for the responsibilities each individual holds.

While I am committed to providing a safe and well-maintained home, my role as a landlord is defined by our lease agreement. It does not extend to solving my tenants' personal crises; their health issues, family struggles, or other misfortunes that may affect their ability to pay rent. My business is to provide housing, not to serve as a safety net for ongoing life challenges that consistently impact financial obligations.

Therefore, I will consistently uphold the terms of our agreement. Rent payments, as per our agreement, are expected on time, every time, regardless of recurring external circumstances.

How Upholding Boundaries Honors God

Some might wonder: "How does enforcing rent payments or standing firm on lease terms honor God?" The answer lies in stewardship, justice, and love. God calls us to manage well what He has entrusted to us (Luke 16:10-12). By setting and enforcing boundaries, we:

- **Demonstrate integrity** – keeping our word and upholding agreements reflects honesty and faithfulness.

- **Protect the vulnerable** – boundaries ensure fairness for all tenants, preventing chaos or resentment that can harm others.

- **Exercise loving stewardship** – caring for property responsibly allows us to serve others well without enabling dependency or creating disorder.

Honoring God isn't about sacrificing yourself to solve every human problem; it's about faithfully managing what He's placed in your hands and creating a space where everyone can thrive under clear, just, and loving expectations.

Creating Your Hard Boundaries (and Sticking to Them)

After walking through the chaos of unclear expectations and emotional decision-making, I knew something had to change. I wasn't just managing properties, I was stewarding peace. And peace requires structure.

I realized that boundaries weren't about being harsh; they were about being holy. They protect your peace, your purpose, and your property. They allow you to lead with clarity instead of reacting with emotion. They create a framework where grace can thrive without enabling dysfunction.

So I sat down and created my own personal policy framework—one rooted in Scripture, stewardship, and sanity. What follows is a simplified version of that process. It's how I moved from emotional reaction to structured response:

1. List Your Non-Negotiables

Decide ahead of time what your "hard lines" are. These are the standards that protect your stewardship and prevent confusion. Examples include:

- Full rent must be paid by the 5th, or a late fee applies.

- No unauthorized occupants or pets allowed.

- Property alterations require written approval.

- Tenants may not withhold rent for maintenance issues.

These aren't just rules; they're reflections of order, care, and clarity.

2. Put It in Writing

If it's not in writing, it's not enforceable. Your lease should reflect every boundary you intend to uphold. This isn't about control, it's about covenant. Written expectations create shared understanding and mutual respect.

3. Respond, Don't React

When a line is crossed, act based on your written policy—not your emotions. This brings peace and fairness to both you and the tenant. It also removes the pressure to "wing it" or make decisions out of guilt or fear.

4. Stay Consistent

What you allow once becomes the expectation. If you waive a late fee without documentation and clear communicative reasoning, tenants may expect it again. Grace can and should be extended where necessary and possible, but it should be rare, clearly framed as an exception, and always documented.

Consistency isn't rigidity, it's integrity. It shows that you honor your word and expect others to do the same.

> If you'd like to go deeper, I've included my full Landlord's Personal Tenant Policy Framework as part of the full 23-template ecosystem. It's the exact structure I use to stay aligned with God's order while managing my properties with

peace and purpose. Use it as a guide, adapt it to your convictions, and let it serve as a compass when emotions try to cloud your decisions.

You'll also encounter a pivotal concept I've come to call Sorting Season™. It's woven throughout this chapter and reflected in several enforcement templates. I'll introduce it shortly, but know this: it's one of the most transformative shifts I've experienced in property management. It marks the moment when accountability reveals alignment, and when structure begins to restore peace.

From "Nice" to Just: Love Requires Limits

For a long time, I thought being a "nice" landlord was the goal. I wanted to be approachable, flexible, and understanding. I thought that was how you reflected Christ, through kindness and compassion. But over time, I learned that love without limits isn't love at all. It's fear dressed up as grace.

Scripture tells us that Jesus was full of grace *and* truth (John 1:14). Many Christian landlords live in grace but forget truth. Or we lean into truth—but forget grace. But love—real, Christlike love—requires both. It requires the courage to say "no," the wisdom to enforce boundaries, and the discernment to know when compassion becomes compromise.

Being "too nice" may feel like mercy, but it can lead to injustice for your other tenants, your family, and even your own mental health. Being lawful doesn't mean being harsh. It means protecting your peace, your purpose, and your property. It means honoring what God has entrusted to you.

It's one thing to set boundaries; it's another to enforce them. That's where the real stretching begins. Because once you start honoring what God has entrusted to you with consistency, things start to shift. Not just in your heart, but in your tenants, your systems, and your entire portfolio.

Sorting Season: When Accountability Shakes the Tree

In social work, there's a foundational concept called Systems Theory. It teaches that when one part of a system changes, it creates ripple effects throughout the whole. I've seen this play out in real estate time and time again. I call it **Sorting Season**, that period when a landlord begins enforcing rules and setting clear boundaries, and everything starts to shift.

Sorting Season doesn't just affect the issue at hand. It changes tenant behavior, household dynamics, and the overall atmosphere of your portfolio. It reveals who's aligned with your standards, and who was only compliant because no one was watching.

Sometimes it starts with a quarterly inspection. Sometimes with a non-payment notice. Often, it's both. And when it begins, you'll see the sorting happen in real time.

I remember one inspection where I discovered an unauthorized dog. The tenant told me it belonged to her brother-in-law and would be gone in a few days. We even discussed the pet agreement and deposit if the dog were to stay. She knew the policy. She understood the boundary.

I've come to call this Sorting Season™—a signature framework I developed after decades of counseling, property management, and pastoral care. It's the moment when accountability shakes the tree and clarity replaces confusion. It's not just a management phase; it's a spiritual shift. And it's become one of the most transformative tools in my stewardship journey.

Fast forward: rent was late. I went to hand-deliver a 7-Day Pay or Quit notice. It was unannounced, and the dog was still there. This wasn't a misunderstanding. It was a choice. I issued a formal warning, highlighted the pet clause in her lease, and gave her five days to remove the animal.

Then there was the midnight runner. This tenant had been violating her lease for months; unauthorized pets, extra occupants, and chronic late payments. I had been lax. I hadn't enforced the standards I'd set. At her inspection, she pushed back, saying the visits felt invasive and made her feel like a Section 8 tenant (even though I treat all tenants equally). Her defensiveness was a red flag. Not long after, she moved out under the cover of darkness, leaving the property a mess. She chose escape over accountability.

Sorting Season teaches you things you can't learn from books or spreadsheets: I've come to see tenant turnover not as a crisis, but as a sorting. When you begin enforcing your lease consistently, when you stop managing from emotion and start leading from conviction, people respond. And their responses reveal more than you might expect.

The solid tenants stay, and often improve when they see you're serious. These are the tenants who were already trying. They may not have been perfect, but they respected the property, paid on time, and communicated with integrity. When they see you enforcing boundaries, they don't resist; they rise. They clean up their act, tighten their habits, and often become even more reliable. Your consistency affirms their efforts. It tells them, *"This is a place of order, and I belong here."* These tenants are your long-term fruit. They're the ones who thrive under structure.

The borderline tenants make a choice; some adapt, others move on. These are the ones who've been teetering. Maybe they've paid late a few times, had a guest stay too long, or pushed the edge of your pet policy. They weren't trying to be defiant; they were testing the limits. When you start enforcing the lease, they feel the shift. Some will adjust. They may apologize, correct the issue, and stay within the lines. Others will decide it's too much work to comply, and they'll leave. Either way, the ambiguity ends. You stop managing uncertainty, and they stop living in it.

The chronic violators self-select out—often suddenly, but ultimately for the better. These tenants were never aligned with your standards. They stayed because no one was watching. They relied on your silence, your leniency, your fear of confrontation. But when you begin enforcing boundaries, they feel exposed. Accountability is uncomfortable for them. So they leave—sometimes quietly, sometimes dramatically. They may ghost you, damage the property, or move out in the middle of the night. It's messy. But it's also merciful because their exit makes room for peace, order, and tenants who respect what you're building.

Sorting Season isn't just about who stays and who goes. It's about who grows. It's about creating an environment where stewardship is honored, not exploited. And yes, it's uncomfortable. But it's also sacred. Because when you lead with clarity, you invite transformation, not just in your tenants, but in yourself.

Before I embraced my role as a steward, I would've panicked: *"My vacancies! My income! My screening process!"* Now, I see it differently: *This is stress leaving. This is peace arriving. This is stewardship in action.*

Sorting Season isn't fun. It's uncomfortable. My tenants were defensive, resentful, and even angry. I wasn't getting invited to any family barbecues, that's for sure. But here's what I know: **accountability is part of stewardship**.

Proverbs 27:23 says, *"Be sure you know the condition of your flocks, give careful attention to your herds."* Knowing the condition of your "flock" of tenants means acting on what you find, even when it's uncomfortable.

Practical Wisdom for Sorting Season

Sorting Season isn't just about enforcing rules; it's about refining your role as a steward. It's the moment when your convictions meet real-world resistance, and your systems get tested. Here's what I've learned through experience, lessons that help you survive Sorting Season with grace and grit:

Document Everything

When emotions run high, documentation becomes your shield. Take photos during inspections. Save texts and emails. Issue written notices, even if you've had verbal conversations. This isn't about being paranoid; it's about being prepared. Documentation protects your integrity, your property, and your peace. It also sends a clear message: *"I'm not just managing—I'm stewarding with intention."*

Stay Consistent

If your lease says late fees apply after the 5th, enforce them. If it prohibits unauthorized pets, follow through. Consistency isn't about being rigid; it's about being reliable. When you waiver, you create confusion. When you follow through, you create clarity. And clarity builds trust, even if it's uncomfortable at first. Your consistency teaches tenants what to expect and reinforces that your boundaries matter.

Don't Take It Personally

Tenants may push back. They may get defensive, emotional, or even accusatory. But their reaction isn't about you, it's about losing comfort. You're disrupting a pattern, and that's hard for people. Don't internalize their discomfort. Stay grounded. You're not being unkind, you're being clear. And clarity is a form of care.

Expect Turnover

Sorting Season often leads to exits. Some tenants will leave because they don't want accountability. Others will leave because they were never aligned with your standards to begin with. Don't panic. Budget for it. Plan for it. See it not as a failure, but as a filter. Turnover is part of the pruning process. It makes room for healthier tenancies and more peaceful management.

Trust the Process

You may lose a few tenants, but you'll gain something far more valuable: alignment. The ones who remain will respect your property, your rules, and your role as a steward. They'll see that you're serious, and they'll respond with stability. Trust that obedience—even when it's uncomfortable—produces fruit. Not always immediately, but always eventually.

Sorting Season is sacred ground. It's where you stop managing from emotion and start leading from conviction. It's where you trade chaos for clarity, guilt for grace, and fear for faith. And yes, it's hard. But it's holy. Because when you honor God with your structure, He honors you with peace.

I've met many landlords who never made it through the Sorting Season. They start with good intentions, hoping to be fair, flexible, and faith-filled—but the emotional toll wears them down. Tenant confusion, inconsistent enforcement, and fear of confrontation slowly chip away at their resolve. Eventually, they stop inspecting, stop enforcing, and settle into survival mode. They collect checks, avoid conflict, and hope nothing breaks.

It's not uncommon. According to the National Apartment Association, property management turnover reached 33% in 2022, well above the national average. And the average tenure for a property manager is just 19.2 months. That's not even two full lease terms before many walk away. The burnout is real. And without boundaries, it's inevitable.

But that doesn't have to be your story.

You don't have to lose your peace to keep your properties. You don't have to choose between compassion and clarity. You can lead with conviction, enforce with grace, and build a business that honors God. Sorting Season is hard, but it's holy. And when you walk through it with structure and surrender, peace follows.

From Lax to Lawful, with Peace

As a Christian landlord, your boundaries are not barriers to compassion—they are the structure that allows compassion to be exercised wisely and without burnout. When you shift from emotionally driven decisions to policy-driven stewardship, you create the space for peace, order, and effectiveness in your business.

This chapter is your permission to stop feeling guilty for enforcing the lease. To stop equating faith with fragility. To start standing on the rock of structure and consistency.

You are not a doormat. You are a steward, called to protect what God has placed in your hands.

And that calling is worthy of boundaries.

Chapter 3 Reflections and Takeaways: From Lax to Lawful—Building Unshakable Boundaries

Key Truths to Carry Forward

Sorting Season isn't just a phase; it's a refining fire. It reveals what you've allowed, what you've avoided, and what you're truly called to uphold. It's where stewardship gets tested and strengthened. These truths will help you carry peace and purpose forward:

- **Boundaries aren't unkind—they're biblical.** God's love is full of grace, but it's also full of order. Boundaries reflect His nature. They protect what's sacred. They create space for peace to flourish. When you enforce them, you're not being harsh, you're being holy.

- **What you tolerate teaches others how to treat your stewardship.** Tenants learn from your silence. If you overlook violations, they assume you're indifferent. But when you respond with clarity and consistency, you teach them that your role is sacred, and that your property is not just a transaction, but a trust.

- **Grace without structure leads to chaos; structure with grace leads to peace.** Many landlords lean into grace and avoid structure, thinking it's more Christlike. But grace without boundaries becomes enabling. Structure with grace, however, brings peace. It allows you to lead with compassion *and* clarity.

- **Being lawful doesn't mean being harsh; it means being faithful.** Enforcing the lease isn't about punishment; it's about protection. It's about honoring what God has placed in your hands. Faithfulness looks like follow-through, even when it's uncomfortable.

- **Sorting Season produces accountability, which leads to healthy stewardship.** When you begin enforcing boundaries, things shift. Some tenants leave. Some improve. Some resist. But through it all, accountability rises. And with accountability comes clarity, peace, and healthier tenancies. Sorting Season is not the end, it's the beginning of order.

Action Steps to Apply

Sorting Season is not just something you survive; it's something you steward. These steps will help you move from emotional reaction to structured response:

1. **Identify three non-negotiables.** What key boundaries do you need to reinforce in your lease, or in your mindset? Write them down clearly and prayerfully. These are your hard lines, rooted in stewardship, not fear.

2. **Audit your lease.** Are your expectations spelled out? Are your consequences enforceable? Vague language invites confusion. Clarity invites peace. Update your lease to reflect the standards you're committed to upholding.

3. **Script your response.** When a tenant crosses a boundary, emotions can rise. Prepare a short, professional response you can use in those moments. This helps you respond, not react. It gives you a voice rooted in grace and structure.

4. **Practice consistency.** Choose one area: late fees, unauthorized occupants, or pet violations, where you will commit to being consistent. Start now. Consistency builds trust and reinforces your role as a steward.

Prayer of Strength

Lord, thank You for being both gracious and just. Teach me to lead like You, full of compassion, yet anchored in truth. Help me honor You with healthy boundaries that reflect my calling as a steward. Give me courage to uphold what's right, wisdom to apply grace, and strength to stay consistent. I trust that peace will follow obedience. In Jesus's name, amen.

Scriptures to Meditate On

- **Corinthians 14:33** *"For God is not a God of disorder but of peace."* Let this remind you that structure is sacred. Peace is born from order.

- **Galatians 6:7** *"Do not be deceived: God is not mocked. A man reaps what he sows."* Your consistency will bear fruit. Sow clarity, and you'll reap peace.

- **John 1:14** *"And the Word became flesh and dwelt among us... full of grace and truth."* Jesus didn't choose between grace and truth; He embodied both. And so can you. Grace without truth leads to chaos. Truth without grace leads to hardness. But together, they form the foundation of godly stewardship. Boundaries rooted in both compassion and justice reflect the heart of Christ. You don't have to compromise one to honor the other.

Chapter 4: The Gates of Discernment: Mastering Screening's Foundation

B efore we move forward, pause and honor the ground you've already reclaimed. You've confronted guilt, clarified your role, and built boundaries that reflect both grace and truth. That's no small feat. Many landlords never make it through that season; they get lost in the chaos, give up on enforcement, and settle for survival. But you've chosen stewardship. You've chosen peace.

Now that your internal framework is firm, your boundaries clarified, your mindset aligned with purpose—it's time to turn outward. Tenant screening is not just a formality; it's the first operational safeguard of your business. This is where your convictions meet the criteria. It's where you stop hoping for good tenants and start selecting them with intention. Screening isn't about being picky; it's about being prepared. It's a strategic and spiritual gatekeeping process that protects your property, your peace, and your purpose.

Now, with a clearer mindset and internal policies rooted in faith, it's time to apply that wisdom to the very threshold of your property: tenant screening. This isn't just a bureaucratic step or a paperwork routine; it's a spiritual discipline, a gate of discernment that protects both the asset and the calling.

Screening is often portrayed as a standard business procedure—and yes, in many ways, it is. But for the Christian landlord, it also reflects a spiritual responsibility. It's where your theology meets your policy. It's where compassion must partner with wisdom, and where grace does not mean carelessness.

The Gate of Discernment: Why Screening Matters

Imagine a shepherd protecting their flock, or a farmer selecting seeds for a harvest. Now, picture a small business owner hiring their first employee; someone who will work directly with customers, handle cash, and represent the brand. Would that owner skip reference checks or dismiss glaring red flags? Of course not. The risks are too high.

Yet many Christian landlords—myself included—have, at times, operated out of fear, pressure, or misplaced grace, skipping essential steps in the name of kindness or urgency. The result? Stress, loss, legal troubles, and, worst of all, a disconnection from the peace and purpose we're supposed to experience in this work.

I once found myself with four vacant properties all at once. Just the thought of the holding costs and pressure to get them filled made me vulnerable to poor judgment. One application stood out: a couple with two small children. They were polite, friendly, and persuasive. They admitted their credit wasn't strong but promised they just needed a chance. I wanted to believe them. They reminded me of my husband and me when we were just starting out. I ignored the red flags: gaps in employment, missing documentation, and a previous eviction that they "explained away."

I gave in to my emotions and yielded to them.

Within months, the same red flags they'd dismissed became my lived reality: late payments, unreturned calls, a broken lease, and property damage. Then, one day, they disappeared. No notice, no goodbye. They left the home in disarray, and me with unpaid rent.

What caught me off guard was what happened a year later. The wife called me out of the blue. Her voice was full of remorse. She asked for forgiveness and said I had been nothing but kind to her and her children. She admitted that she and her husband had separated and that she had made many mistakes. I appreciated the call—I genuinely did. Then, a few weeks later, she called again. She'd seen another one of my homes listed and asked if she could apply. She offered to pay two months' rent and a deposit up front.

I was floored.

Even after breaking the lease and walking away, she thought I would rent to her again. I politely told her the property was no longer available and wished her well. But the deeper lesson for me was this:

even kind people can make poor tenants, and emotional appeal can never replace clear evidence of responsibility.

Not every screening story is dramatic, but each carries weight. One applicant begged me to allow their large dog, promising it was well-behaved. I caved, against my own policy. Within weeks, neighbors complained about barking, fences were chewed, and the floors were damaged. When they moved out, the repair costs were extensive. It wasn't just a lesson in pet policies; it was a reminder that bending your standards invites disorder.

Then there was the property that slowly became overrun with parked, non-working cars. At first, it was one. Then two. Eventually, it looked like a used car lot. Neighbors called to complain. Code enforcement got involved. The tenant always had a reason why a tow truck was "on the way." In truth, they were simply living in chaos, and I had enabled it by not clearly defining the rules up front. Once I started including language about vehicle limits and maintenance expectations in my leases—and enforced them—the issues declined.

These experiences taught me that tenant behavior isn't random; it reflects what they believe is acceptable. If your screening and onboarding processes are lax or vague, you'll spend the rest of the lease managing confusion, conflict, and control issues.

Discernment Is Spiritual and Practical

What does discernment look like in real time? It's pausing when you feel rushed. It's checking references, verifying income, and asking awkward follow-up questions. It's being willing to walk away from an applicant who doesn't align, even when the mortgage is due. It's remembering that discernment is not judgment, it's stewardship.

Proverbs 13:16 says, "Every prudent man acts with knowledge, but a fool flaunts his folly." We act with knowledge, not hunches, not pressure, not pity. And Matthew 10:16 calls us to be "wise as serpents and innocent as doves." This is not just poetry, it's policy.

Screening is your frontline boundary. It's the filter that determines whether the next year will be peaceful or painful. And the gatekeeper is you.

When created with faith, wisdom, and clarity, this gate protects your property, your peace, your finances, and your ministry as a Christian landlord.

Chapter 4 Reflections and Takeaways: The Gates of Discernment, Mastering Screening's Foundation

Key Truths to Carry Forward

Tenant screening is more than policy; it's stewardship. It's the first gate of protection for your property, your peace, and your purpose. When you screen with discernment, you're not just checking boxes; you're honoring what God has entrusted to you.

- **Discernment is not harsh or judgmental. It's wise, spiritual protection.** You're not called to be suspicious, you're called to be wise. Discernment allows you to see beyond charm, urgency, or emotion. It helps you recognize patterns, inconsistencies, and potential risks. It's not about rejecting people, it's about protecting peace.

- **Pressure to fill a vacancy is not an excuse to ignore red flags.** Vacancy can create financial stress, but rushing into a lease with the wrong tenant creates far more damage. Don't let urgency override wisdom. Red flags are not inconveniences; they're invitations to pause. God's peace often speaks through hesitation.

- **Even good people can be poor tenants, and that doesn't make you unkind for saying no.** This is one of the most brutal truths for compassionate landlords. You may meet someone who's sincere, struggling, and kind—but still not qualified. Saying no doesn't mean you lack grace. It means you're honoring your stewardship. You can pray for someone without housing them.

- **Clarity up front prevents conflict later.** Ambiguity breeds confusion. When your screening criteria are clear, consistent, and communicated, you reduce misunderstandings and protect relationships. Tenants may not agree with every policy, but they'll respect consistency. And respect is the foundation of healthy tenancy.

Action Steps to Apply

1. **Revisit your screening criteria.** Do your current standards reflect both wisdom and legality? Are they written down and consistently enforced? If not, revise them. Your criteria should be strong enough to guide decisions and clear enough to withstand pressure.

2. **List three red flags you've ignored in the past.** What patterns do you tend to overlook out of empathy or fear? Late payments, vague references, incomplete applications? Name them. Own them. Then commit to not repeating them.

Discernment grows when you learn from what you've tolerated.

3. **Clarify the "non-negotiables."** Decide in advance what will always disqualify an applicant: prior evictions, insufficient income, incomplete documentation, or dishonesty. These are not punishments, they're protections. When you know your hard lines, you won't second-guess them under pressure.

4. **Write your screening mantra.** Create a short phrase to center you when emotions rise or urgency creeps in. Something like: *"Peace is better than pity.""Clarity is kindness.""I'm protecting what God entrusted to me."* Post it near your desk or wherever you review applications. Let it anchor you.

Prayer of Discernment

Father God, give me eyes to see beyond what's presented and ears to hear beyond what's said. Let me not be led by fear, guilt, or pressure, but by Your Spirit. Teach me to be wise as a serpent and gentle as a dove. Help me steward every property—and every decision—with discernment, courage, and compassion. In Jesus's name, amen.

Scriptures to Meditate On

- **Proverbs 13:16 –** *"Every prudent man acts with knowledge, but a fool flaunts his folly."* Let your decisions be rooted in knowledge, not impulse.

- **Matthew 10:16** – *"Behold, I am sending you out as sheep in the midst of wolves, so be wise as serpents and innocent as doves."* Discernment is spiritual wisdom in action. Jesus knew we'd face deception, manipulation, and pressure. Being wise as serpents means recognizing what's beneath the surface— reading motives, spotting red flags, and making strategic decisions. Being innocent as doves means staying grounded in integrity. Discernment helps you navigate tough situations without losing your peace or your witness.

- **Proverbs 4:23** – *"Above all else, guard your heart, for everything you do flows from it."* Your heart is the gatekeeper of your stewardship. It filters your motives, your reactions, and your discernment. If your heart is cluttered with fear, offense, or greed, your decisions will reflect that. Guarding it means protecting your peace, staying rooted in truth, and filtering every opportunity through prayer. Wise stewardship begins with a well-protected heart.

- **Proverbs 27:23** – *"Be sure you know the condition of your flocks, give careful attention to your herds."* Stewardship requires active oversight. Don't assume things are running smoothly; inspect your properties, review your finances, and check in on your partnerships. Staying informed is not micromanagement; it's faithfulness.

When you pay attention, you protect what God has entrusted to you.

Chapter 5: The Practical Blueprint: Steps to Finding Your Ideal Tenant

The Practical Blueprint: Steps to Finding Your Ideal Tenant

T enant screening is the foundation of wise landlording. It's not about paranoia, it's about prudence. It's the act of setting clear boundaries before problems arise, of protecting peace before it's ever disrupted. When done well, screening becomes a filter for alignment, not just a checklist for eligibility. It's where stewardship meets strategy.

This chapter is your blueprint, a step-by-step guide to applying discernment in real time. Because while spiritual clarity is essential, practical systems are what carry it forward. You've built the internal framework. Now it's time to operationalize it.

Step 1: The Initial Inquiry and Pre-Screening Questions

Before you ever set foot on the property with a prospective tenant, implement a basic pre-screening process. It's one of the simplest ways to save time, energy, and heartache, because once emotions get involved, it becomes harder to make objective decisions. A friendly phone call, a warm demeanor, or a compelling story can cloud your judgment if you haven't anchored your criteria in advance. Pre-screening helps you stay grounded. It allows you to assess alignment before investing time. And most importantly, it reinforces that your role is not just to fill a vacancy, but to protect what God has entrusted to you.

Tenant screening begins long before the showing. It starts with how you present your property and how you filter initial interest. The goal is not to attract the most applicants, it's to attract the right ones. That means being unapologetically clear about your standards. Clarity isn't harsh; it's kind. It protects both you and the applicant from wasted time, mismatched expectations, and future conflict. When you advertise with precision, you're not just marketing a rental; you're stewarding a boundary.

Advertise Clearly

Your listing should communicate essential requirements without leaving room for guesswork. Don't hide conditions, hoping they'll "work themselves out later." If pets aren't allowed, say so explicitly. Many people love their pets, but if you've just laid new carpet or worry about damage, being clear upfront protects everyone from future conflict. A no-pets policy, plainly stated, is far easier than later discovering an unauthorized "emotional support iguana" in your rental.

Another nonnegotiable is income. Spell it out clearly: "Income must be at least 3x rent." Few things are more frustrating than realizing, after move-in, that your tenant was never financially able to meet rent consistently. This guideline sets realistic expectations and prevents heartache for both parties.

Credit score is another filter. My baseline is typically 600. But numbers don't tell the whole story. A medical debt weighing down a score is different from reckless retail credit card spending. Look at the patterns, not just the points. What you want is evidence of responsibility, not perfection.

And then there's eviction history. Personally, I don't accept tenants with prior evictions, so I say that outright. It's far better to be clear on the front end than to be surprised later.

Phone or Email Questionnaire

Even with a detailed listing, most applicants won't read it. That's a small red flag in itself, because it often foreshadows a tenant who won't read the lease later either. That's why I use a simple phone or email questionnaire to filter quickly. The questions are straightforward:

What's your desired move-in date?

Why are you moving?

How many people will live in the home, and what's their relationship to you?

Do you have pets?

What's your approximate monthly household income?

Have you ever been evicted or broken a lease?

Are you willing to complete a background and credit check?

I automate these screening questions so applicants complete them before accessing the full application or ordering credit and background checks. This protects your time and theirs. If someone isn't willing to answer basic questions, they're not ready for the next step. Automation also ensures consistency; every applicant is treated the same, and every process is repeatable.

Real-Life Scenario: The Charming Dodger

I once spoke with an incredibly charming applicant who sidestepped every question about income and employment. I brushed it off, thinking I'd collect the details on the formal application.

Guess what? She never submitted one: wasted time, wasted energy. The lesson stuck, charm is not a qualification. This might seem like a trivial point, but it IS a red flag and can cost you much frustration and income if the charming dodger finds their way into one of your properties and begins to dodge the rent. That experience taught me something I now consider foundational: *screening is not about personality, it's about patterns.* A warm smile and a compelling story might feel reassuring, but they're not indicators of reliability. If someone sidesteps basic questions, it's not just awkward; it's instructive. Every interaction before the application is part of the screening process. And if you're paying attention, you'll see the signs early. Charm without clarity is a red flag. Don't ignore it.

The Rush to Move In

Another common red flag is urgency. I've made the mistake of letting tenants move in early because of an "emergency" or emotional story. Almost every time, those situations became my problem within weeks. If a tenant isn't prepared for their own move, they're not going to respect your systems once inside your property. Stick to your timeline, not theirs.

The Instant Cash Offer

And then there's the fast-cash offer—another test of your resolve, "I can meet you today—I got the cash in my hand!"

Tempting? Yes. Wise? No. People who want to skip your process at the beginning will skip your rules later, too. Trust this: the way they enter is the way they'll behave. Always stick to your full screening protocol, no exceptions.

Biblical Application

Proverbs 21:5 reminds us: "The plans of the diligent lead surely to abundance, but everyone who is hasty comes only to poverty." Careful planning at the pre-screening stage isn't busywork; it's protection. Diligence here shields your peace, your property, and your purpose.

Step 2: Show the Property (Only After Pre-Screening)

With pre-screening in place, I now conduct far fewer showings, and that's by design. Gone are the days when I'd meet anyone who asked to tour the property. That approach drained my time, blurred my boundaries, and opened the door to applicants who were never truly viable.

Pre-screening filters out the lookers from the serious contenders. It spares you from showing the home to someone whose lease isn't up for five more months and is "just browsing." It weeds out the applicant who sees the rent is $1,400 but can only afford $1,000, and hopes you'll make an exception. It also protects you from the person who bristles at basic screening questions, calling them an invasion of privacy. If someone resists structure early, they'll resist it later.

By the time I show a property, I've already confirmed alignment on income, timeline, household size, and willingness to complete background checks. That means the showing becomes less about convincing and more about confirming. It's a chance to observe, to listen, and to discern—without pressure.

Remember: **you're not just offering a space, you're inviting someone into your stewardship.** Show the property with clarity, not desperation. And never skip the process just because someone seems eager. Eagerness without alignment is not a green light; it's a caution flag.

Step 3: The Comprehensive Application

Once a prospective tenant has passed pre-screening and viewed the property, the next step is a **fully completed application for every adult who will live in the home**. This is where structure meets stewardship. You're not just collecting data; you're confirming alignment.

No Incomplete Applications

An incomplete application is a red flag. It may signal carelessness, dishonesty, or disregard for instructions. Be polite but immovable: *"We can't move forward until everything is filled out."* If someone won't follow basic directions now, they won't follow your lease later. Clarity here protects you down the road.

Application Fee

At this stage, it's appropriate—and wise—to charge a non-refundable application fee. This isn't about profit; it's about process. The fee covers the cost of credit and background checks, but it also serves a deeper purpose: it signals commitment. If someone hesitates at a modest fee after clearing pre-screening, it's often a sign they aren't serious about renting. And if they're not serious now, they won't be serious later; when rent is due, when rules are enforced, or when repairs require cooperation.

This fee is a filter. It helps you separate the curious from the committed. It also reinforces that your business is structured, not casual. You're not just offering a place to live; you're stewarding a property with purpose.

Two important notes here:

- **I never charge more than what it actually costs to run the reports.** Overcharging isn't just unethical, it's unwise. It erodes trust and invites scrutiny. Keep it clean, keep it fair, and keep it documented.

- **By the time someone reaches the full application, they've already completed the automated screening questions.** That early structure ensures you're only reviewing serious, qualified applicants. It protects your time and theirs, and it reinforces consistency; every applicant is treated the same, and every process is repeatable.

Charging an application fee may feel uncomfortable at first, especially if you're used to informal processes. But remember: **stewardship requires structure.** And structure, when paired with grace, leads to peace.

This quick, yet thorough review helps me determine whether the applicant meets my criteria without wasting their money or my time. I've never been comfortable with people spending unnecessarily if they don't qualify in the first place. That's why clarity and alignment must come before the application, not after.

What Your Application Should Include

Your rental application is your first filter; it sets the tone for the relationship and establishes professionalism from the very beginning. A thorough application not only gathers information but also signals to the tenant that you take your role seriously.

Think of it as a stewardship tool. You're not just collecting data; you're looking for patterns, consistency, and integrity. Every field should serve a purpose. When crafted with clarity, your application becomes a boundary that protects both parties from future conflict.

Here's what I include in every application:

Full Legal Name and Contact Information (for Each Adult)

Every adult occupant must complete their own application, even if only one person plans to sign the lease. This isn't just a technical requirement; it's a boundary rooted in wisdom. When someone lives in your property, they're part of the household dynamic. Their behavior, financial habits, and respect for structure will directly impact the peace and stability of your rental. That means every adult must be known, vetted, and accountable.

If someone refuses to apply, they're refusing accountability. And if they resist accountability before move-in, they'll resist it during tenancy; when rent is due, when rules are enforced, or when conflict arises.

I once had a situation where the leaseholder looked perfect on paper: excellent credit, stable income, and a respectful demeanor. But because I required separate applications for all adults, I discovered that their live-in partner had a history of evictions, unpaid rent, and disputes with previous landlords. Had I skipped that step, I would've unknowingly allowed someone into the home who had a proven pattern of instability.

And here's the truth: once they're living there, it's no longer just about the leaseholder—it's about the household. If the partner influences financial decisions, disrupts the peace, or refuses to leave, you're dealing with a legal and emotional entanglement that's hard to unwind. Courts don't care who signed the lease; they care who lives in the unit. You can't evict half a household. You can't enforce peace with one signature.

By catching that early, I was able to decline the application before signing anything. No eviction process. No property damage. No months of unpaid rent. Just a clean boundary, enforced through structure.

This is why I say: every adult must apply. No exceptions. It's not about being rigid, it's about being responsible. You're not just managing a property. You're stewarding a space where peace, order, and purpose are meant to dwell.

Date of Birth and Photo ID

Request a copy of a valid government-issued ID. This isn't just about confirming identity; it's about protecting yourself legally. If a tenant defaults and you need to pursue legal action, having verified identification is essential. I've seen cases where landlords couldn't even serve proper notice because they didn't have the tenant's legal name or birthdate on file. Don't skip this step.

Current and Previous Addresses

Patterns matter. A tenant who's moved five times in two years may be dealing with instability, or may be fleeing unresolved issues. Ask yourself: is this someone who will stay long enough to build trust and consistency? If the moves are job-related, that's one thing. But if they're all within the same city, it may signal conflict, eviction, or poor planning.

Reason for Moving

This question often reveals more than people intend. "Job transfer" suggests stability. "My landlord was unfair" might be true, but it also might be a pattern. If every move is blamed on someone else, take note. I once had an applicant who said they were leaving because "the landlord was too strict." That told me everything I needed to know about how they'd respond to boundaries in my property.

Landlord Contact Information

Don't just call the most recent landlord; go one step back. The current landlord may be eager to offload a problem tenant and give a glowing review just to get them out. But the previous landlord? They have no stake in the outcome. I've had conversations where the first landlord said, "Great tenant," and the second said, "They left damage, paid late, and argued constantly." That second call saved me thousands.

Employment History

Include employer names, positions, income, and supervisor contact information. You're looking for stability, not just income. A tenant who's had five jobs in a year may struggle to meet rent consistently. I once had an applicant with a high-paying job, but they'd only been there two weeks and had left their last three positions abruptly. That's not just a financial risk, it's a behavioral one.

Income Verification

Documentation matters. Pay stubs, tax returns, or bank statements help you verify that the income claimed is real and consistent. I've had applicants say they earn $5,000/month, but their bank statements showed deposits of $2,200. That's not a rounding error, it's a misrepresentation. Trust, but verify.

Vehicle Information

License plate numbers and photos may seem excessive, but they're invaluable for recordkeeping. If a car is abandoned, parked illegally, or involved in a dispute, you'll need to know who it belongs to. I once had a tenant whose guest parked in another tenant's spot repeatedly. Having vehicle records helped resolve the issue quickly and fairly.

Pet Information (if applicable)

Collect breed, weight, age, vaccination records, and even a photo. This isn't just about rules; it's about safety and liability. A "small dog" could mean a 15-pound terrier or a 60-pound pit bull. I've had tenants describe their pet as "quiet and well-behaved," only to discover it was untrained and aggressive. Clarity upfront prevents conflict later.

Other Occupants

Require names and ages of everyone, including minors. Be mindful of tenants who underreport occupants or plan to use your unit for extended family or subletting. I once approved a tenant expecting three residents, only to find a whole extended family of eight squeezed into two bedrooms. That wasn't just a violation of the lease; it was a safety issue. Overcrowding strains plumbing, increases wear and tear, and creates tension with neighbors.

In addition, include sections for:

- **Emergency Contact**

  Ask for the name, relationship, and phone number of someone who can be reached in case of an emergency. This isn't just a formality; it's a safeguard. If something happens to the tenant, or if you need to reach someone due to a serious issue (like abandonment or hospitalization), you'll be grateful to have a trusted contact on file. I've had situations where a tenant disappeared mid-lease, and the emergency contact was the only way to get clarity.

- **Background and Credit Check Authorization**

  Include a clear statement that authorizes you to run background and credit checks. This protects you legally and ensures transparency. Make sure the language is direct: *"By signing below, I authorize the landlord to obtain credit and background reports for screening purposes."* If someone refuses to sign this, that's your answer: they're not ready for accountability.

- **Acknowledgment of Lease Terms**

  Even before the lease is signed, it's wise to include a summary of key terms, rent amount, due date, pet policy, occupancy limits, and maintenance expectations. Ask the applicant to initial or sign that they've read and understood these terms. This prevents the "I didn't know" conversation later. Clarity now is kindness later.

- **Declaration of Accuracy**

  Include a statement that everything provided is true to the best of their knowledge, and that falsifying information may result in denial or termination of tenancy. This sets a tone of integrity. If someone hesitates to sign this, it's a red flag. You're not just collecting facts, you're inviting honesty.

- **Optional Comments Section**

  Give applicants space to explain unusual circumstances. Maybe they had a temporary job gap, a medical issue that affected their credit, or a past eviction they've learned from. This section allows for nuance without compromising structure. It also shows that you're fair, but firm. You're willing to listen, but you won't ignore patterns.

We'll explore this more deeply later in the book, but I feel compelled to say it plainly here: Don't be in such a hurry to move a tenant in that you ignore visible red flags. Do your due diligence. Every detail in your process serves a purpose. Skipping even one can cost you dearly.

Before we move on, I want to pause and speak to something deeper. It's easy to get caught up in the mechanics of screening: verifying documents, checking references, following the steps. But behind every checkbox is a decision that affects your peace, your property, and your purpose. And if you're not careful, urgency will tempt you to compromise the very boundaries you've worked so hard to build.

I speak from experience. There was a season when I hated making mortgage payments with no rent coming in. The pressure was real, and it pushed me to lease quickly to people I should have never approved. I ignored red flags because I needed relief. But relief without discernment is a trap.

Rushing to fill a vacancy—just to stop the financial bleeding—**ate up my profits and my peace.** The tenants I approved out of urgency ended up costing me in repairs, unpaid rent, conflict resolution, and emotional bandwidth. What looked like a quick win became a slow leak.

Those decisions cost me dearly: sleepless nights, strained relationships, and the emotional toll of conflict I could've avoided. I learned that **urgency is a poor substitute for wisdom.** A vacant unit is hard, but a misaligned tenant is harder. One drains your patience; the other drains your purpose.

Now, I slow down. I listen. I let structure do the heavy lifting. I trust the process I've built. Because every detail in your screening isn't just a task, it's a boundary that protects your margins, your mission, and your mind.

Profit without peace isn't success. Stewardship means protecting both.

Step 4: Verifying the Details

Now your role shifts to investigator. **Trust, but verify.** The goal isn't to unfairly disqualify anyone; it's to confirm consistency. You're not looking for perfection; you're looking for alignment. Does the story match the evidence? Does the applicant's life reflect the kind of stewardship you want in your property?

This step is where discernment meets diligence. Every detail you verify is a boundary that protects your peace.

The Big Three Reports

Credit Check: When reviewing credit reports, pay attention to late payments, collections, bankruptcies, liens, or high debt loads. Compare the applicant's stated income against their obligations. Does the math make sense? Use discretion, as not all debts are equal. A medical bill in collections tells a different story than a string of unpaid credit cards.

Don't hesitate to ask respectful, clarifying questions. A tenant with nothing to hide will often appreciate the opportunity to explain and provide the information you need. At the same time, someone who reacts defensively or takes offense may not be the right fit for your property. You're not interrogating, you're clarifying. And clarity is kindness.

Criminal Background   When reviewing an applicant's criminal background, pay close attention to convictions involving violence, drugs, or property crimes. It's important to exercise discernment while remaining fully compliant with fair housing laws.

Having worked as a forensic therapist, I know that not all convictions are created equal. A single offense from years ago may not reflect who someone is today. But a pattern of disregard for others' safety or property? That's a red flag. If an applicant seems promising despite past convictions, it's appropriate and respectful to ask questions that clarify the context before making a decision.

Eviction Records   Even an eviction filing—not just a judgment—is a serious red flag. Always use a service with national reach, not just local. When it comes to evictions, I personally do not tolerate them. My approach is simple: **if a tenant forces one landlord to go to court for removal, they will inevitably force me to do the same.**

Evictions are costly, stressful, and disruptive for both the landlord and the community. This is why I take screening seriously and enforce lease terms consistently from day one. Grace is important, but structure is non-negotiable.

Direct Verifications

Employment: Call the employer directly, don't just rely on the contact provided. Match pay stubs or W-2s against the income claimed on the application. Look for consistency, not just numbers. A tenant who earns well but changes jobs every few months may still be a financial risk.

Landlords may need a release-of-history form signed by the applicant, especially when dealing with apartment complexes or management companies. Don't stop at one reference; call multiple past landlords. Ask questions that reveal patterns, not just surface-level behavior:

- "How would you describe their payment habits?"

- "Would you rent to them again?"

- "Were there issues with pets, noise, or unauthorized occupants?"

- "Did they leave with outstanding debt?"

- "How did they handle maintenance needs?"

These questions aren't just about data—they're about discernment. You're listening for tone, hesitation, and consistency. You're not just verifying facts—you're confirming character.

Other Red Flags to Watch For

These aren't always deal-breakers, but they are signals. When you see them, slow down. Ask questions. Verify. Because what you ignore now may cost you later.

Inconsistent dates across documents. If the move-in date on the application doesn't match the lease end date from the previous landlord, or if employment dates don't line up with pay stubs—pause. These inconsistencies may be innocent, but they may also signal dishonesty or instability. I've seen applicants list a job they hadn't started yet, just to boost their income on paper. That's not just misleading, it's a breach of trust.

"Landlords" who don't exist online. If someone lists a private landlord, check for a digital footprint. Is there a business listing, a rental website, or even a basic online presence? If not, ask for backup, like lease agreements or utility bills. I once had an applicant list a "landlord" who turned out to be a cousin helping them fabricate a reference. When I pressed for real documentation, they withdrew their application.

Applicants refusing to provide references. Transparency is a baseline. If someone won't provide employer or landlord references, that's a red flag. A qualified tenant should be able to offer at least one solid reference without hesitation. If they say, *"I don't want you calling my job,"* **or** *"My last landlord was crazy,"* listen carefully. You're not just screening for income, you're screening for character.

Excessive urgency or pressure ("I need this place tomorrow!"). Urgency is often a mask for instability. When someone pushes hard for immediate move-in, it's worth asking why. Are they being evicted? Did they burn a bridge elsewhere? Are they trying to bypass your process? Stewardship means slowing down, even when someone else is speeding up. You're not just offering shelter; you're offering structure.

Emotional appeals without documentation: "I just went through a divorce." "I lost my job, but I'm getting back on my feet." "I'm a good person, I just need a chance." These stories may be true, and they may deserve compassion. But compassion without documentation is risky. If someone can't provide proof of income, rental history, or identity, they're asking you to carry a burden they haven't earned. You can be kind without being careless.

At the end of the day, your goal isn't perfection, it's **consistency**. When the facts align, the patterns make sense, and the applicant demonstrates transparency, you can proceed with greater confidence that they can be trusted with your property.

Discernment isn't suspicion, it's stewardship. You're not just protecting your investment. You're protecting your peace.

Biblical Application

"The naive believe everything, but the prudent man considers his steps."

— Proverbs 14:15

This verse isn't just a warning; it's a framework for how we steward decisions. Screening tenants isn't about suspicion or fear. It's about wisdom. Prudence means pausing long enough to verify, to ask questions, to confirm that what's presented aligns with the truth. It's the difference between reacting and responding.

In this process, you're not just protecting your property—you're protecting your peace. The naive landlord believes every story, skips verification, and hopes for the best. The prudent landlord considers each step, each document, each reference. They understand that stewardship requires structure.

God doesn't call us to paranoia—but He does call us to discernment. When you verify details, you're not being harsh—you're being faithful. You're honoring the responsibility He's entrusted to you. Every step you take in truth is a step away from chaos and toward peace.

The Fruits of Prudent Stewardship

Even the most thorough screening process can't eliminate every problem—but it will protect you from many unnecessary ones.

Prudent stewardship bears fruit in every area of your work as a landlord.

It protects your investment and well-being. Careful decisions guard not only your property, but your peace of mind. You sleep better knowing you've done the work upfront.

It preserves your peace. A sound, consistent, and spiritually aligned blueprint, one that reflects your business outlook, values, and biblical convictions, gives you confidence even when conflict arises. You're not scrambling; you're anchored.

It secures your profitability. Responsible tenants bring fewer repairs, fewer vacancies, and far fewer evictions. Your margins stay intact because your boundaries are clear.

It upholds your purpose. You're not simply running a business; you're stewarding homes. You're contributing to your community. You're honoring God through integrity, wisdom, and structure.

In the end, this is about more than filling a vacancy. Each screening is an opportunity to build your house upon the rock, not the sand. Through diligence, you establish a business that glorifies

God operates with wisdom and becomes a blessing to those you serve.

A full, detailed application and tenant prescreening plug-and-play templates—fully editable, clearly structured, and ready for immediate use—complete with criteria, red flags, and follow-up protocols—are

included in the digital template collection. These resources are available individually or as part of the full 23-template ecosystem designed to support faith-driven landlords with clarity and peace. Details on how to access the templates will be provided in Chapter 8 and at the end of this book.

Chapter 5 Reflections and Takeaways: The Practical Blueprint—Steps to Your Ideal Tenant

Key Truths to Carry Forward

These truths aren't just practical, they're spiritual. They anchor your process in wisdom, protect your peace, and reflect your calling as a steward.

- **Screening is stewardship.** This isn't just about paperwork; it's about protecting what God has entrusted to you. Every decision you make reflects your care for the property, your peace of mind, and your purpose in the community.

- **Your process is part of your testimony.** Professionalism isn't separate from faith; it's an extension of it. When your systems are clear, consistent, and fair, they reflect spiritual maturity and integrity. Your business becomes a witness.

- **Pre-screening protects your peace.** A simple script and clear criteria filter out misalignment early. You avoid emotional entanglement and stay grounded in structure. Peace begins with preparation.

- **Rushed applicants bring rushed problems.** Urgency is not a reason to skip protocol. When someone pressures you to move faster than your process allows, that's a red flag. Slow down. Protect your margins.

- **The application is a boundary test.** How someone handles the screening process reveals how they'll handle rules, expectations, and accountability. If they resist structure now, they'll resist it later.

- **Consistency is your shield.** Applying the same standard every time protects you from confusion, compromise, and accusations of bias. It builds trust and reinforces your authority.

- **Faith includes due diligence.** Trust God, but verify everything. Faith doesn't mean skipping steps. It means walking in wisdom, asking hard questions, and honoring truth.

- **Discernment is spiritual and practical.** You're not just running a business, you're stewarding lives. Slow down. Pray. Ask for clarity. Then proceed with peace, knowing you've done the work.

Action Steps to Apply

1. **Create or Review Your Pre-Screening Script.** Prepare a simple list of questions to ask before scheduling showings.

Practice using them with clarity and confidence. Let your tone be firm, kind, and consistent.

2. **Review and Standardize Your Application Process.** Ensure every adult submits a complete application with all required documentation. No exceptions. This protects your structure and your peace.

3. **Evaluate Your Verification Methods**. Commit to calling employers and previous landlords. Don't rely on surface-level information; verify every detail. Your diligence is your defense.

4. **Write Your Boundary Statement.** Keep a written reminder of your nonnegotiables visible. This helps you stay consistent when pressure rises. *Example: "I will not skip steps or rush decisions, no matter the pressure."*

Steward's Prayer

Lord, thank You for entrusting me with this property. Help me to steward it with wisdom, courage, and consistency. Give me eyes to see what's true, ears to hear what's hidden, and a heart rooted in Your peace. Let every applicant be treated with fairness and grace, but let every decision be guided by Your wisdom. In Jesus's name, amen.

Scriptures to Meditate On

- **Proverbs 22:3** *The prudent sees danger and hides himself, but* *the simple go on and suffer for it."* Discernment is protection. Wisdom sees what emotion overlooks.

- **Proverbs 20:18** *"Plans are established by counsel; by wise guidance wage war."* Your screening process is strategic, not random. Wise counsel—through mentors, policies, and prayer—builds a system that protects your peace and your property. Don't skip steps. Build with intention.

- **Titus 1:7** *"Since an overseer manages God's household, he must be blameless—not overbearing, not quick-tempered, not given to drunkenness, not violent, not pursuing dishonest gain."* You're managing more than property; you're stewarding influence. Your process should reflect integrity, patience, and fairness. When your standards are clear and consistent, your leadership becomes a testimony.

Chapter 6: The Sacred Agreement: Building a Thorough Lease

A thorough lease is not just a legal document; it's a spiritual safeguard, a boundary of stewardship, and a tool for peace. Without it, even well-intentioned tenants can create costly confusion.

In the world of social work, where I served for over thirty years, there's a guiding principle: "If it's not documented, it didn't happen." That truth doesn't just apply to case notes; it applies to property management with even greater weight. In this realm, the rule becomes: "If it's not in the lease, it doesn't apply." This isn't cynicism, it's clarity. Verbal agreements are fragile. They fade, shift, and often vanish under pressure. But a written lease? That's your documented truth. It's the anchor when memory fails, the shield when conflict arises, and the blueprint when resolution is needed.

Research supports this. According to RCP Management, a firm with over 40 years of experience managing community associations and recognized as both an Accredited Management Organization (AMO) and an Accredited Association Management Company (AAMC), a well-written lease is *"the cornerstone of effective property management,"*

111

offering legal protection, clarifying expectations, and minimizing risk. While their focus is on community associations, the principle applies across the board: structure protects peace.

I learned this firsthand. A tenant once signed the lease, paid the deposit, and for ten months, paid rent and utilities, but never moved in. No furniture. No boxes. No physical presence. The yard—his responsibility—grew wild, drawing complaints. It became clear he was using the address for reasons unrelated to actual residency: perhaps mail, business registration, or probation compliance. Then, without warning, he left, owing two months of unpaid rent and the property damaged.

The problem? Not just at the end, but throughout this tenancy, there were gaps in the lease. Specifically, it didn't define **occupancy.** It didn't address **abandonment** when rent was paid, but the tenant was absent. It didn't clarify what **neglect** looked like when no one was physically present. These gaps left me vulnerable, unable to enforce maintenance, reclaim the property, or even prove the tenant had breached the agreement.

That wasn't the only time vague lease language left me exposed. In another situation, unsure of how to proceed, I consulted a real estate attorney for guidance. Again, the issue pointed back to the lease. Yes, my lease mentioned abandonment, property condition, and occupancy, but the language was vague. It required tenants to inform me if they'd be away for more than 14 days, but it didn't define *failure to occupy*, or address *clear signs of neglect* and *property vulnerabilities*. Even basic issues, like installing security features or entering the property, became legal gray areas.

The attorney stressed that the lease was too loosely written. Some areas weren't addressed at all. And because the tenant was still paying rent and maintaining utilities, I had limited leverage. As the lease neared its end, I sent a timely non-renewal notice. The tenant stopped paying. Days after the lease expired, I entered the property and found a television on the floor and a bedframe still in the box, no signs of actual residency.

I immediately sent the 14-day abandoned property notice, outlining how to retrieve the items, where they were being held, and for how long. The tenant ignored the notice, broke down the door, retrieved his property, and later emailed me to acknowledge it.

Yes, some tenants aren't the wisest. But the real issue wasn't just his behavior—it was the lack of clarity in my lease. It took time, legal guidance, and repair work, but I was eventually made whole. Still, much of this could have been avoided if my lease had explicitly defined:

What constitutes *occupancy*

What triggers **abandonment**

What permissions exist for ***property entry***

What responsibilities remain during **non-residency**

How **neglect** is measured when rent is still being paid

This is why a thorough lease matters. It's not just paperwork, it's protection. It defines who is responsible for what, how long, under what conditions, and with what consequences. It outlines expectations for occupancy, maintenance, communication, and resolution. It prevents assumptions, fosters mutual respect, and safeguards the asset God has entrusted to you.

For the Christian landlord, this isn't about being overly legalistic; it's about being loving through structure. Scripture reminds us in 1 Corinthians 14:40, *"Let all things be done decently and in order."* A clear lease reflects that order. It honors both parties. It creates peace before problems arise.

As we move into the breakdown of lease essentials, remember this: your lease is your ministry in writing. It's where stewardship meets structure. It's where clarity becomes kindness. And it's where your business begins to reflect the wisdom and integrity of the One who entrusted it to you.

Essential Elements of a Sacred Lease Agreement

Admittedly, I've become a by-the-lease kind of landlord. And from reading the section above, I hope you understand why. A lease isn't just a formality; it's a boundary of peace. It's the structure that protects your property, your purpose, and your sanity.

The only thing more important than having a thorough lease is this: **follow-through**. A lease only works if you enforce it. If you skip steps, bend rules, or make exceptions without documentation, you weaken the very structure you built to protect yourself.

Think of your lease as a **comprehensive guide**, a written covenant that addresses every foreseeable aspect of the tenancy. Every line, every clause, every addendum serves to document an agreement. It ensures that *"if it's not in the lease, it doesn't apply"* works for you—not against you. It provides clarity, consistency, and enforceability.

This is where stewardship meets structure. You're not just protecting your investment—you're modeling integrity. You're creating a framework that reflects your values, your expectations, and your commitment to order.

Amendments and Addenda

Any changes after the lease is signed, such as a change in occupancy, pet ownership, or responsibilities, **must be agreed upon in writing** and followed up with a signed addendum. Verbal agreements are not enough. This protects both parties and ensures that your lease remains the final authority.

Parties and Property Identification

- **Lessor and Lessee Information:** Clearly identify all parties.

List the full legal names of every adult who will reside in the property and is legally bound by the lease. This is critical for legal enforceability and future communication.

- **Occupancy List:t** Include a complete list of all authorized occupants, including children, by full name. This ensures clarity on who is permitted to reside on the premises and helps prevent unauthorized occupants or subletting.

- **Property Description:** Provide the full address of the rental property, including the unit number if applicable. Include any specific areas covered by the lease (e.g., garage, yard, storage units) to avoid confusion later.

Term of Tenancy

- **Lease Start and End Dates:** Explicitly state the exact dates the lease begins and ends. These dates must be documented precisely to avoid ambiguity or disputes.

- **Lease Type:** Specify whether it's a fixed-term lease (e.g., 12 months) or a month-to-month agreement. This determines how the lease renews and how termination is handled.

- **Renewal and Termination Clauses** Outline the notice period required for non-renewal by either party and the process for lease renewal (e.g., new lease signing, month-to-month conversion). If a notice period isn't specified here, it won't apply, and you'll have no legal ground to enforce it.

These details may seem basic, but they are foundational. When dates are vague, lease types are unclear, or renewal terms are missing, confusion is inevitable and costly. I've seen landlords lose months of rent or face legal delays simply because a lease didn't specify how and when it ends. As a steward, your role is to eliminate ambiguity before it becomes conflict. A clearly defined term of tenancy honors both parties, sets expectations from day one, and gives you the legal and spiritual footing to manage transitions with confidence and grace.

Financial Terms

Money may be a sensitive topic, but in property management, **clarity is kindness**. Financial terms must be spelled out with precision. Vague language leads to disputes, delays, and legal vulnerabilities. As a steward, your goal is not just to collect rent, it's to create a structure that honors both parties and reflects integrity.

- **Rent Amount** State the exact monthly rent amount in both numerical and written form (e.g., "$1,200.00 – One Thousand Two Hundred Dollars"). No verbal agreements on rent adjustments should ever be made without a signed addendum.

- **Due Date:** Specify the precise day of the month rent is due (e.g., "Rent is due on the 1st of each month"). If this isn't clearly stated, it becomes negotiable, and that's a risk you don't want.

- **Payment Method:** Clearly define acceptable payment methods (e.g., online portal, direct deposit, check). If you don't list a method, a tenant could argue that any form of payment—including cash or third-party apps—is acceptable.

- **Late Fees** Detail any late fees, including the amount, when they apply (e.g., after a 3- or 5-day grace period), and how they accrue. Ensure these comply with local laws. If not documented, late fees cannot be charged, no matter how justified they feel.

- **Security Deposit** State the exact amount of the security deposit, how it will be held (e.g., in an escrow account, as required by law), the conditions for its return (e.g., no damages, property clean), and the timeline for its return after move-out. Every condition for retention or return must be explicitly written and aligned with state/local regulations.

- **Other Fees:** Clearly list any other permissible fees, such as insufficient funds (NSF) fees, amenity fees, or administrative charges. If it's not listed, it can't be enforced.

Financial clarity isn't just about protecting your income; it's about protecting your peace. When expectations are documented, disputes are minimized. When terms are enforceable, stewardship becomes sustainable. And when your lease reflects both legal wisdom and spiritual integrity, your business becomes a testimony of order, fairness, and faith.

Utilities and Services

Utilities may seem like a minor detail, but they often become the source of major disputes, especially when expectations aren't clearly defined. If the lease doesn't specify who pays for what, tenants may assume utilities are included, delay transfers, or dispute charges. This creates confusion, financial strain, and unnecessary tension. As a steward, your role is to eliminate ambiguity. By documenting utility responsibilities and transfer timelines, you protect your margins, prevent miscommunication, and ensure that both parties operate with transparency. Clear terms here reflect not just professionalism, but spiritual integrity.

- **Tenant vs. Landlord Responsibility** Clearly itemize which utilities (e.g., electricity, water, gas, trash, internet) are the tenant's responsibility and which are the landlord's. Be specific, don't assume anything is "understood."

- **Transfer Timeline:** Specify the exact date by which utilities must be transferred into the tenant's name (e.g., "All applicable utilities must be transferred into the tenant's name within 72 hours of the lease start date"). If not documented, responsibility becomes ambiguous and enforcement becomes difficult.

- **Included Services**: If any services are included in the rent (e.g., lawn care, pest control, Wi-Fi), list them clearly and define the scope. This prevents assumptions and ensures tenants understand what is—and isn't—covered.

- **Shared Utilities or Metering**: If utilities are shared (e.g., duplexes, multi-unit homes), explain how costs are divided and how payments are tracked. Include formulas or flat-rate agreements if applicable.

Property Use and Maintenance

A lease doesn't just define financial terms; it governs how the property is used, cared for, and respected. This section is where stewardship becomes visible. If these expectations aren't clearly documented, tenants will default to assumption, and assumption is the enemy of peace. Every clause here protects the integrity of your property and the clarity of your relationship.

- **Occupancy Limits:** State the maximum number of occupants allowed, aligning with fair housing laws. This prevents overcrowding and protects the property's condition and zoning compliance.

- **Restrictions on Use:** Outline rules regarding illegal activities, commercial use, excessive noise, or alterations to the property without permission. These rules are unenforceable if not in writing, and unenforced rules invite chaos.

- **Tenant Maintenance Responsibilities:** Clearly define what maintenance the tenant is responsible for (e.g., light bulbs, smoke detector batteries, yard care, pest control, trash removal, keeping drains clear). Provide guidelines for reporting needed repairs. This is where my earlier experience taught me a hard lesson: if yard care isn't listed, it often won't happen.

- **Lawn Care and Property Condition** The tenant is responsible for regular lawn maintenance and yard care, including mowing, watering, trimming, and removal of debris to keep the property in a neat and presentable condition. Failure to maintain the yard may be considered a breach of the lease.

- **Vehicles:** No abandoned, inoperable, or unregistered vehicles are permitted on the property at any time. All vehicles must be properly licensed, operable, and parked in designated areas. Vehicles violating this policy may be subject to towing at the tenant's expense.

- **Property Abandonment** Property abandonment occurs if the tenant is absent from the property for more than 14 consecutive days without prior written notice to the landlord and fails to pay rent during this period. Abandonment also includes situations where the property is left in a state of neglect, such as failure to maintain yard care or the presence of

121

abandoned vehicles. Upon determination of abandonment, the landlord may take possession of the property in accordance with your state's law.

- **Landlord Maintenance Responsibilities** State what the landlord is responsible for maintaining (e.g., structural integrity, major appliances, plumbing, electrical systems). This ensures tenants know what to expect and where their responsibilities end.

- **Entry to Property:** Clearly outline the conditions under which the landlord can enter the property (e.g., emergency, repairs, inspections) and the required notice period, complying with state/local laws. This protects both parties and prevents misunderstandings.

- **Property Alterations:** Explicitly state that no alterations (e.g., painting, installing fixtures, mounting TVs) can be made without the landlord's prior written consent. This preserves the property's condition and prevents costly repairs.

- **Pets:** If pets are allowed, incorporate a Pet Addendum that covers pet fees/deposits, breed/weight restrictions, vaccination requirements, tenant responsibilities for pet waste/damage, and rules regarding noise or nuisance. If no pets are allowed, state this explicitly. A "no pets" policy is meaningless if it's not written in the lease **and enforced**.

- **Smoking Policy:** Clearly state whether smoking is prohibited inside the property and/or on the premises. Include language about consequences for violations and how smoking-related damage will be assessed.

This section may feel exhaustive, but that's the point. Stewardship requires structure. When expectations are clear, enforcement is simple. When boundaries are documented, peace is preserved. And when your lease reflects both legal wisdom and spiritual integrity, your property becomes a place of order, not chaos.

Default and Remedies

- **Breach of Lease:** Define what constitutes a breach (e.g., nonpayment of rent, unauthorized occupants, property damage, violation of rules). Without clear definitions, proving a breach becomes difficult, and enforcement becomes subjective.

- **Notice to Cure or Quit:** Outline the process and timelines for notifying the tenant to remedy a breach or vacate the property. This must align with your state's laws (e.g., a 7-day notice period for nonpayment of rent). Without this clause, your hands may be tied when issues arise.

- **Attorney's Fees and Collection Costs** Include language stating that the tenant is responsible for legal fees or collection costs if they default. These costs are often unrecoverable if not explicitly documented in the lease.

Lease Addenda and Disclosures

- **Lead-Based Paint Disclosure** is required by federal law for properties built before 1978. This is not optional—include the form and ensure it's signed.

- **Mold Addendum:** Consider an addendum outlining tenant responsibilities for mold prevention and prompt reporting. This protects both parties and reinforces shared accountability.

- **Move-In/Move-Out Checklist.** While technically a separate document, reference it in the lease. It's essential for documenting property condition and protecting your right to withhold from the security deposit if needed.

- **Rules and Regulations**: For multi-unit properties or homes with shared spaces, attach any community rules or house-specific expectations as an addendum. These must be referenced in the lease and signed to be enforceable.

- **Other Addendums (Smoking, Parking, Pets, etc.)** Ensure all relevant addenda—whether for smoking, parking, pets, or amenities—are listed in the lease, attached, and signed by all parties. If an addendum isn't referenced and signed, its contents may not be legally binding.

The Lease as a Tool for Peace

For the Christian landlord, a thorough lease isn't merely a legal shield, though it certainly serves that purpose. It's an act of proactive love and good stewardship. It means you've thought through potential friction points and provided clear guidance. It minimizes surprises for your tenant and protects your investment from avoidable damage or financial strain.

This diligence, rooted in wisdom, empowers you to operate with a clear conscience and less anxiety, knowing you've done your part to establish a fair and transparent relationship. When everything is clearly documented, arguments dissolve, and the path to peace becomes clearer, because *"if it's not in the lease, it doesn't apply"* applies to both landlord and tenant.

Remember: A lease is only as good as its enforcement.

Biblical Application

Just as we are called to be diligent in our work (Proverbs 12:24) and wise in our dealings (Ephesians 5:15), a meticulously crafted lease is a practical embodiment of these principles. It demonstrates integrity and foresight, ensuring that both parties understand their roles and responsibilities within this sacred agreement. It fosters an environment where consistency and accountability thrive, allowing your property to be a blessing to your tenant and a well-managed asset that honors God.

The complete lease plug-and-play template —fully editable, clearly structured, and ready for immediate use in this chapter—including occupancy definitions, abandonment clauses, and enforcement language— is part of the digital template collection. You'll find it available individually or within the full 23-template bundle created to help landlords steward with structure and integrity. Instructions for accessing the templates will be shared in Chapter 8 and at the conclusion of this book.

Chapter 6 Reflections and Takeaways: From Casual to CovenantEmbracing the Lease as Sacred Stewardship

Key Truths to Carry Forward

- **A lease is not just paperwork. It's a covenant that reflects your role as a faithful steward.** A lease isn't merely a legal document; it's a reflection of your values, your leadership, and your spiritual posture. You enter into a covenant that calls both parties to honor what's been entrusted. As a landlord, you model integrity by creating agreements that are fair, firm, and rooted in truth. Stewardship begins with structure, and the lease is your first act of order.

- **Clarity is an act of love; confusion invites conflict.** Ambiguity breeds anxiety. When expectations are vague, both you and your tenants are left guessing, and that guesswork often leads to tension, resentment, or legal disputes. But when you communicate clearly, you offer peace and dignity.

- **Legal precision protects spiritual peace.** You can't separate the spiritual from the structural. A well-written lease, a documented policy, or a signed addendum isn't just legal armor; it's a spiritual safeguard. It allows you to sleep at night, knowing you've done your part to uphold order. Legal precision doesn't mean rigidity—it means readiness.

- **Holding tenants accountable honors both the property and the people.** Accountability isn't punishment, it's protection. When you enforce your lease with consistency and grace, you're not just defending your investment; you're honoring the people involved. You're saying,"I care enough to uphold what we agreed to." Accountability creates safety, restores trust, and reinforces the dignity of the covenant.

Action Steps to Apply

1. Review Your Lease Prayerfully. Read through your lease as a covenant, not just a contract. Where could it be clearer, stronger, or more reflective of your values?

2. Enforce What You Write. If a policy isn't enforced, it's just a suggestion. Choose one lease clause you've let slide, and begin holding the line with consistency and grace.

3. Educate Your Tenants. Consider a short walk-through or Welcome email that highlights key lease expectations in plain language. Help tenants understand, not just sign.

4. Document Everything. Start using lease addenda for unique situations (e.g., pets, guests, repairs). Keep signed copies of all modifications for future protection.

Prayer of Integrity

Lord, thank You for being a covenant-keeping God. Help me reflect on your integrity by creating leases that are honest, fair, and firm. Give me the courage to be clear, the wisdom to anticipate conflict, and the grace to communicate expectations with love. May every document I write honor You as the ultimate Landlord and Owner of all things. In Jesus's name, amen.

Scriptures to Meditate On

- **Psalm 15:4 – "...who keeps an oath even when it hurts, and does not change their mind."** *"If a policy isn't enforced, it's just a suggestion."* This echoes the Psalmist's call to keep our word, even when it's uncomfortable.

- **Ecclesiastes 5:5 – "It is better not to make a vow than to make one and not fulfill it."** Your lease is a vow in writing. Let it reflect what you're truly willing to uphold.

- **Matthew 5:37 – "Let your 'Yes' be 'Yes,' and your 'No,' be 'No'; anything more comes from the evil one."** Clarity in your lease is not just legal, it's spiritual. It protects both parties from confusion and compromise.

Chapter 7: Partnering with Professionals: Working with Contractors and Vendors

P roperty management isn't just about finding tenants and collecting rent; it's about actively managing the entire life cycle of the tenancy and being prepared for the inevitable challenges that arise. This chapter moves us from foundational principles and policy-setting to the practical, day-to-day realities of being a landlord, all while keeping our focus on diligent and faithful stewardship.

Working with Contractors: The Ultimate Win/Win (and Lessons from the Field)

It is virtually impossible to maintain a long-term rental portfolio without frequently dealing with—and often relying on—a network of contractors, handymen, and appliance repair professionals. These individuals are crucial partners in protecting your asset and ensuring your tenants have a safe, well-maintained home. But if this area isn't managed with intentionality and wisdom, it can become one of the most expensive and emotionally draining parts of your stewardship.

Here's the tension: **Their goal is to get paid. Your goal is not to lose money.** At first glance, that seems straightforward. But if the relationship isn't grounded in clarity, covenant, and mutual respect, it can quickly become adversarial.

I've worked with talented, professionally driven contractors—and when expectations are clear and communication is strong, it's a beautiful partnership. The work gets done, the property is protected, and everyone walks away satisfied. That's the win/win.

But I've also had my share of nightmare scenarios—contractors who overpromised, underdelivered, disappeared mid-project, or left behind damage and drama. When boundaries aren't set and stewardship is compromised, things can get ugly fast. What starts as a simple repair can spiral into financial loss, emotional strain, and spiritual frustration.

That's why this chapter matters. Because contractor relationships aren't just logistical—they're spiritual. They reflect your leadership, your diligence, and your commitment to honoring what God has entrusted to you.

In fact, a 2023 industry report found that over 80% of contractors have experienced payment disputes or delays, often due to unclear expectations, missing documentation, or verbal-only agreements. That statistic doesn't just reflect contractor frustration; it signals landlord vulnerability. When expectations aren't written, boundaries blur. And when boundaries blur, stewardship suffers.

One of the most deceptive traps in contractor relationships is what I call the polished pitch. The gift of gab is so perfected in some trades that you can walk away from a conversation feeling confident, impressed, and ready to hand over your keys—without a single document signed. But here's the truth: their word is not their bond. And while it may sound good, stewardship demands more than sound; it demands substance.

My early experiences taught me that the true cost of labor, or what various trades charged, was often a mystery. Everyone claimed they could do everything. They had "a guy" for this, "a crew" for that, and "years of experience" in between. But far fewer truly delivered on doing the right thing. I learned the hard way that good intentions don't guarantee good outcomes. And that trust, without verification, is not faith,it's presumption.

I've sat across from contractors who spoke with such confidence and charisma that I felt foolish for even asking for paperwork. But I've also paid dearly for that misplaced trust, through botched jobs, broken promises, and expensive repairs that could've been avoided with one slow, discerning pause... and due diligence.

Stewardship Requires Discernment

Discernment isn't suspicion; it's wisdom. Proverbs 18:17 says, *"The first to speak in court sounds right; until the cross-examination begins."* The proverb uses the analogy of a court of law to illustrate the importance of impartiality and gathering all the facts before forming a decision. In today's terms, the first contractor to pitch may sound perfect until you ask for licenses, references, and a written scope of work.

Here's what I now practice:

Slow down. Don't let urgency override wisdom.

Listen beyond the pitch. Ask questions that reveal character, not just capability.

Verify everything. Licenses, insurance, references, and written agreements aren't optional; they're spiritual safeguards.

The Perils of Undue Trust and Cutting Corners

One of my most painful lessons came with a new property acquisition, which I acquired from a family member. In my desire not to appear untrusting, I took her word on the property's condition, not realizing she, in turn, was taking someone else's word. I bypassed my due diligence entirely and did not conduct a professional home inspection.

She assured me the house had a new roof; in fact, I even remembered when the work was being done. However, it turned out she had been misinformed; the supposed "new roof" was not new at all. When a leak appeared, I initially dismissed it as an old issue, failing to pay proper attention. Had I acted as a good steward and done my due diligence with a professional inspection, I would have discovered the truth and avoided the costly necessity of putting on a truly new roof, only after significant water damage had already ruined new floors and walls.

That early mistake highlighted several common pitfalls:

Hiring relatives purely to "help family." While the intentions are good, assuming someone can do the work simply because they say they can—or because their father was a master electrician—doesn't mean they inherited the skill, the standards, or the stewardship. Family ties don't guarantee professional results. And when you skip vetting in the name of loyalty, you often end up with substandard work, awkward conversations, and damaged relationships, both personal and professional.

Cutting corners to "save a buck." The allure of a cheaper quote is strong, but my experience taught me that short-term savings often lead to long-term headaches. I've spent multiple "bucks" to correct what would have cost one "buck" if done right the first time. Quality and durability are paramount for long-term rentals.

Failing to check references, licenses, and insurance, I didn't verify the integrity of their professed credentials. This oversight can expose you to immense liability if a contractor is uninsured and gets injured on your property, or if their work is faulty and damages the home.

The "No Contract" Catastrophe. Perhaps the most infuriating lesson involved a contractor who was merely bush hogging the yard. Despite the seemingly simple task, he parked a heavy truck directly on top of the septic tank, breaking the lid. Of course, he denied it, despite obvious tire tread imprints. Because there was no contract specifying general property care, prohibited parking areas, or responsibility for damages, I was left to purchase and install a new septic lid at my own expense. This underscores that even for seemingly minor jobs, a basic agreement can save you significant time, money, and frustration.

Establishing a Win/Win Partnership: Principles of Diligent Stewardship

My journey through these costly lessons has forged a new approach, one focused on building win/win relationships with contractors, grounded in transparency, clear expectations, and mutual respect. This isn't just good business; it's an act of diligent and wise stewardship.

Here's what I've learned is nonnegotiable for success:

Thorough Vetting Is an Act of Prudence

Check References. Don't just ask for names, call them. Ask specific questions about reliability, quality, communication, and how the contractor handled problems when they arose. You're not just verifying skill; you're testing character.

Verify Licenses and Insurance. For any significant work, always confirm that the contractor holds a valid professional license (if required for their trade) and carries both liability and workers' compensation insurance. Request a Certificate of Insurance directly from their insurer, not just a verbal assurance.

Obtain Multiple Bids. For substantial projects, get at least two or three detailed bids. This helps you understand market rates, compare scopes of work, and spot red flags. It's not about shopping for the cheapest, it's about shopping for clarity and value.

Clarity Through Comprehensive Contracts

Don't accept flimsy contracts. For anything beyond a minor repair, insist on a written agreement that includes:

..Full Scope of Work: A detailed description of what will be done, what materials will be used, and what is excluded.

..Start and Completion Dates: Clear timelines, with agreed-upon penalties for significant delays if appropriate.

..Payment Arrangement: Define when payments are due, ideally tied to milestones, not just upfront or all at the end. Avoid paying large sums before work begins.

..Who Will Be on Property: List the names of individuals or teams who will access your property during work hours.

..How Unforeseen Issues Are Addressed: Include a process for handling unexpected discoveries that may impact cost or timeline.

..Warranties: Clarify what guarantees the contractor provides for their work. For example, a fortified roof certificate saved me 25% on property insurance across three different properties.

..Site Conduct & Property Protection: Explicitly state rules regarding smoking, alcohol use, and property care, such as avoiding septic tanks, designated parking areas, and cleanup requirements. These details prevent costly oversights like the septic tank damage I experienced.

And here's why this matters: I once contracted a partial fence installation—$3,000 total. Against my usual practice, I paid an $800 deposit up front. Then the contractor disappeared. Ghosted me for months. I filed in small claims court and later discovered this was a pattern; he had defrauded others and was eventually jailed. I never had to appear in court, but nearly two years later, I received a check in the mail reimbursing my deposit, filing fees, and more. It was a rare resolution—but the stress, delay, and vulnerability were real. And it all could've been avoided with firmer boundaries and better documentation.

Security and Trust: Knowing Who Has Your Keys & What They Share

Always know exactly who has access to your property. For major work, consider collecting photo IDs from lead contractors or anyone who will hold keys.

Be prepared to change locks after a significant project, especially if multiple contractors had access or if you have any reservations. I once discovered a contractor had set up a sleeping bag and television, essentially living at the property and even inviting his girlfriend over at night. It was a profound breach of trust and a stark reminder to maintain clear boundaries around access and use.

Confidentiality Matters

Your property is a business asset. Contractor conversations should stay professional and focused. I've had contractors casually share details with curious neighbors or potential "drive-by" tenants, leading to unwanted inquiries and misinformed gossip. While often harmless, it's best to maintain professionalism and direct all external questions to you.

Focus on Quality and Durability

Shift your mindset: focus less on "saving a buck" and more on the quality of work and durability of materials. A higher upfront cost for a reputable, skilled professional using quality materials will almost always save you money and headaches down the road. It's not just a repair, it's an investment in the longevity and value of your stewardship.

Cultivating the Win/Win

Finally, ensure that you get your money's worth, and that the contractor gets theirs too. Fair pricing for their expertise and timely payment upon satisfactory completion builds trust. When you treat contractors with respect, communicate clearly, and pay fairly for good work, you foster loyalty and attract the best talent—vital partners in your long-term success as a faithful steward.

Tenants as Contractors: Proceed with Discernment

The thought often crosses a landlord's mind: *"What if my tenant could do that repair? It would put money in their pocket, and I'd save on contractor fees. It's a win-win, right?"*

On the surface, it sounds efficient. And in some cases, with the right tenant, a clear skill set, and a tightly written addendum, it can work. I've rented to tenants who are licensed contractors, handymen, and remodeling professionals. When handled with discernment, structure, and strict boundaries, these arrangements can be mutually beneficial.

But here's the key: this is not casual or informal work. If you choose to go this route, it must be treated with the same level of professionalism and legal clarity as any other vendor relationship. That means:

Absolutely no rent substitutions. Labor should never be exchanged for rent. Payment must be separate and properly documented to avoid legal and tax complications.

Use a written addendum. Clearly define the scope of work, payment terms, liability coverage, and expectations for conduct and communication.

Prohibit tenant-to-tenant involvement. The working tenant should never manage or coordinate with other tenants on your behalf.

Maintain clear boundaries. They are tenants first. Their work must not give them special access, authority, or influence beyond the job at hand.

That said, I've personally found these arrangements to be a bridge too far. My early experiences—where I allowed lines to blur, quickly taught me the dangers of mixing tenant and contractor roles. What seemed like a friendly, cost-saving solution often led to professional headaches, financial losses, and strained relationships.

Stewardship requires clarity. And clarity means keeping roles distinct, unless you're fully prepared to manage the legal, relational, and operational complexity that comes with blending them.

Why It's Generally a Practice to Avoid: A Stewardship Perspective

While hiring a tenant for repairs may seem convenient, it introduces risks that often outweigh the benefits. Here's why this practice is generally discouraged from the lens of wise and diligent stewardship:

Massive Liability Exposure

This is the biggest red flag. If your tenant is injured while working, whether falling off a ladder or cutting themselves, you could be held liable. Most tenants do not carry workers' compensation or adequate liability insurance. Your property insurance likely won't cover injuries sustained during labor. This risk alone often outweighs any perceived savings.

Blurred Boundaries and Lack of Accountability

When the person responsible for paying rent is also responsible for completing work, the relationship becomes complicated. How do you address shoddy workmanship? How do you enforce deadlines if they're behind on rent? The professional boundary between landlord and tenant erodes quickly.

I've experienced this firsthand. I once used a tenant for certain work. Later, when I pressed for rent, he texted to complain that other tenants were getting their homes fixed up but not his. That moment revealed how quickly resentment, perceived favoritism, and blurred roles can undermine a clear financial agreement. I never hired him again.

Quality Control and Expertise

Is your tenant truly qualified? Many are "handy," but professional-grade repairs, especially plumbing, electrical, or structural, require licenses, training, and experience. Accepting amateur work can lead to costly repairs, code violations, and safety hazards. That's not just a financial risk, it's a failure of stewardship.

Legal Complications for Eviction

If a dispute arises or the tenant stops paying rent, they may claim they "paid" through labor. This can complicate eviction proceedings and make it harder to prove nonpayment in court. It directly undermines the clarity and enforceability of your lease.

Perception and Fair Housing

Offering special arrangements to some tenants but not others can raise questions of fairness, and in some cases, even touch on fair housing concerns. Even with good intentions, inconsistent practices can be misinterpreted. Consistency is a cornerstone of justice and professionalism.

The Steward's Best Practice

While the desire to help a tenant or save money is understandable, the wise steward recognizes when a shortcut introduces greater risk.

Maintain Clear Separation. Tenants pay rent and follow the lease. Contractors perform agreed-upon work. Keep these roles distinct.

Pay for Services Separately. If you do hire a tenant for a specific task— and only if they are licensed and insured—treat it as a separate business transaction. Use a formal contract, verify insurance, and pay them directly. Never offset rent with labor.

As Christian landlords, we are called to be *wise as serpents and innocent as doves* (Matthew 10:16). That's not a call to suspicion; it's a call to spiritual discernment. In the realm of contractors, it means setting clear boundaries and avoiding unnecessary risk, even when a solution seems compassionate, convenient, or cost-effective.

Greed doesn't always show up as malice; it often disguises itself as efficiency. It whispers, *"Just let the tenant fix it. You'll save money."* Presumption doesn't always feel reckless; it often feels relational. It says, *"I trust them. We've had good conversations."* And the easy road doesn't always look dangerous; it often looks like relief. It tempts you to skip the contract, ignore the insurance, and hope for the best.

But stewardship isn't built on shortcuts. It's built on structure. It's not just about protecting your property; it's about protecting your peace, your testimony, and your ability to lead with integrity.

Your properties are valuable assets entrusted to you. They are not just buildings; they are assignments. And every decision you make around them reflects your leadership and your spiritual posture. When you blur the lines between tenant and contractor, you risk more than money; you risk confusion, resentment, and legal entanglement that could have been avoided with one moment of clarity.

Your properties are not just investments, they're assignments. And stewardship means honoring God not only in what you build, but in how you manage it. Set clear boundaries. Avoid unnecessary risk. And let your diligence reflect the One who entrusted it to you.

Chapter 7 Reflections and Takeaways: From Haphazard to Honorable - Partnering with Professionals in Stewardship

Key Truths to Carry Forward

- **Stewardship isn't passive; it requires proactive partnership and due diligence.**

  Faithful stewardship means actively managing what God has entrusted to us. It's not enough to hope things go well; we must plan, prepare, and partner wisely. Just as Nehemiah carefully selected workers and assigned tasks to rebuild Jerusalem's walls (Nehemiah 3), we too must be intentional in choosing who we work with and how we oversee the work.

- **Sloppy shortcuts today create spiritual and financial burdens tomorrow.**

  Cutting corners may save time or money in the moment, but it often leads to costly repairs, broken trust, and spiritual unrest. Stewardship demands excellence, not expedience. Think of the parable of the wise and foolish builders, one built on rock, the other on sand. Only one foundation endured the storm (Matthew 7:24-27).

- **Contracts create clarity. Boundaries protect peace. Trust must be verified, not assumed.**

Written agreements aren't signs of distrust; they're tools of wisdom. They protect both parties and prevent confusion. Even God made covenants with His people, clear, binding promises that defined expectations and built trust.

- **Honoring labor and expecting excellence is part of faithful management.**

God values work and those who do it. When we honor the labor of others—through fair pay, clear expectations, and respectful treatment—we reflect His justice and dignity. Excellence isn't perfection; it's doing all things as unto the Lord (Colossians 3:23).

Action Steps to Apply

1. **Vet Before You Regret:** Think of this as your stewardship screening. Ask for references, verify credentials, and ensure insurance is in place. Proverbs 18:17 reminds us that "the first to speak seems right, until someone comes and cross-examines." Due diligence is a spiritual discipline.

2. **Standardize Your Agreements:** Even small jobs deserve clarity. A written agreement is a modern-day covenant; it sets expectations, timelines, and accountability. It's a way to love your neighbor by preventing future conflict.

3. **Audit Your Access:** Stewardship includes security. If you wouldn't hand over your wallet, don't hand over your keys without accountability. Luke 16:10 says, "Whoever can be trusted with very little can also be trusted with much."

4. **Separate Roles Wisely:** Mixing roles, like tenants doing repairs, can blur boundaries and erode trust. Stewardship means maintaining clear lines of responsibility. Jesus didn't ask His disciples to build the temple; He knew their calling and kept roles distinct.

Prayer of Wisdom

Lord, You are a God of order, justice, and protection. Help me to reflect Your character in the way I partner with those who work on the homes You've entrusted to me. Teach me to lead with integrity, to choose contractors carefully, and to honor labor without compromising wisdom. May I never cut corners at the cost of peace. Strengthen my discernment, shield me from deception, and help me steward each partnership as a reflection of You. In Jesus's name, amen

Scriptures to Meditate On

- **Luke 14:28 –** *"Suppose one of you wants to build a tower. Won't you first sit down and estimate the cost?"* Before starting any project, whether a renovation, investment, or partnership, create a clear plan and budget. Preparation prevents regret.

- **Proverbs 22:3 – *"The prudent see danger and take refuge, but the simple keep going and pay the penalty."*** Don't ignore red flags. If something feels off with a contractor, agreement, or situation, pause and investigate. Wisdom avoids unnecessary loss.

- **Timothy 5:18 – *"The worker deserves his wages."*** Pay contractors and workers fairly and promptly. Honor their labor as part of your witness and stewardship.

Chapter 8: Managing the Tenancy Life Cycle and Challenges

B eyond managing the property's physical needs, actively managing the tenancy itself—from initial move-in to final move-out—is crucial for peace of mind and protecting your investment. When handled with diligence and clear procedures, this entire cycle minimizes disputes and maximizes efficiency. A well-managed tenancy is not just about collecting rent; it's about fostering a respectful, professional relationship with tenants, setting clear expectations, and maintaining consistent communication. Each phase of the tenancy, screening, onboarding, maintenance, and exit, offers a chance to reinforce stewardship, reduce liability, and build long-term value.

Neglecting the relationship and process side of renting out property can lead to confusion, legal trouble, and a lot of unnecessary stress. It's not just about fixing things when they break or collecting rent; it's about managing the whole experience with care and consistency. When landlords stay organized, communicate clearly, and treat tenants with respect, they create a smoother, more positive environment for everyone involved.

Good property management means staying ahead of problems instead of waiting for them to blow up. That includes setting expectations early, checking in regularly, and handling issues before they grow. It's about being fair but firm, making sure tenants feel respected while also keeping standards high. When both sides know what to expect and feel heard, it's easier to avoid conflict and keep things running well.

Move-In Procedures: Setting the Stage for Success

The move-in process is more than just handing over the keys; it's your chance to clearly document the condition of the property and make sure the tenant understands what's expected of them. Taking time to do a walk-through, snap photos, go over the lease, and have both parties sign a condition report helps avoid confusion later. It's a fair way to protect both sides and shows that you're serious about doing things the right way.

This first step sets the tone for everything that follows. When tenants see that you're organized, respectful, and clear, they're more likely to treat the property and the agreement with the same level of care. It also gives you a chance to build trust, answer questions, and make sure everyone's on the same page. Starting strong helps prevent problems down the road and reminds everyone that good rental management is about more than just the building; it's about clear communication, mutual respect, and keeping things running smoothly.

Detailed Move-In Inspection Report

This is your primary defense against future disputes over damages. Before the tenant moves in, complete a thorough, room-by-room inspection.

Move-In Documentation: Your First Line of Defense

One of the best ways to avoid disagreements later is to thoroughly document the property's condition before the tenant moves in. This step might feel tedious, but it's your strongest protection if there's ever a dispute about damage when the lease ends.

Use a Checklist: Walk through the property room by room and check everything, walls, floors, appliances, fixtures, windows, doors, and even closets. A detailed checklist helps make sure nothing gets missed.

Take Photos and Video: Make use of that cell phone camera, capture timestamped photos and a video walkthrough of every space, including close-ups of any existing wear and tear. This visual record can be a lifesaver if questions come up later.

Tenant Sign-Off: Have the tenant review and sign the inspection report within the first 24 to 48 hours of moving in. Give them a copy for their records. It might seem like a small step, but it can make a big difference when sorting out issues like nail holes or scuffed floors at move-out.

This process shows tenants that you're organized and fair, and it sets the expectation that you'll hold them accountable for the condition of the property. It also helps avoid "he said, she said" situations later on.

Security Deposit Handling: Don't Skip This Step

It's important to follow your state's laws when it comes to collecting and handling security deposits, but just as important is the timing. One lesson I learned was to trust a tenant to pay the security deposit after signing the lease. She signed electronically and even scheduled a time for me to come pick up the payment. But when I showed up, she told me she didn't have the full amount and asked to split it over several months. At that point, the lease was already signed, and I was stuck. She technically had a legal claim to the unit, but I didn't have the deposit in hand. It created confusion and left me financially exposed before the tenancy even began.

To make matters worse, this same tenant—despite having a solid income—ended up paying rent late 9 out of 12 months and received two 7-day pay or quit notices. Looking back, the deposit issue was an early warning sign. If someone can't meet the basic move-in requirements, it's often a preview of how the rest of the lease will go.

Now, I ask upfront during screening: "Will paying the full security deposit be a problem?" If there's any hesitation, I take it seriously. I've made it a firm policy: no lease gets signed, and no keys are handed over until the full deposit is paid. It's not about being strict. It's about protecting your property, your time, and your peace of mind—but also protecting the tenant from stepping into an arrangement they may not be able to manage or maintain. When expectations are clear and financial readiness is confirmed upfront, it sets both parties up for success. If a tenant struggles to meet the basic move-in requirements, it's often a sign that the lease may become a burden for them down the road. By setting firm but fair standards, you're not just guarding your investment; you're helping prevent a situation that could lead to stress, conflict, or hardship for the tenant as well.

Best Practice: Always collect the full security deposit before or at the same time as the lease is signed—and definitely before handing over keys or giving access to the property. If a tenant can't pay the full amount, consider requiring a co-signer or politely declining the application.

Move-Out Procedures: Protecting Your Investment and Preventing Disputes

The move-out process is just as important as the move-in when it comes to protecting your property and avoiding disagreements over the security deposit. This is where all the documentation you gathered at move-in really proves its value.

Give Clear Instructions: As soon as the tenant gives notice to move out—or if you, the landlord, decide not to renew the lease—send written move-out instructions right away. This document should include a checklist of what the tenant needs to do before leaving (like cleaning and trash removal), and it should clearly state the scheduled date for the final walk-through. Providing this in writing helps avoid confusion, sets expectations, and keeps the process smooth for both sides.

Do a Final Walk-Through: If possible, schedule a final inspection with the tenant present on the day they move out or shortly after. This gives you both a chance to walk through the property together and talk through any concerns.

Compare to Move-In Records: Use your original inspection report, photos, and videos to compare the current condition of the property to how it looked at move-in. This helps keep things objective and fair.

Document Any New Damage: Take new timestamped photos or videos of anything that's damaged beyond normal wear and tear. If the tenant is there, talk through any potential deductions from the deposit. If they've already left, do a full inspection and include your findings in the final accounting.

Security Deposit Return & Accounting

Make sure you follow your state's laws about when and how to return the security deposit or provide a breakdown of any deductions. In my state, for example, the law allows up to 60 days, but it's best to send it as soon as you've completed the final inspection and received any repair estimates or invoices.

Always include a detailed, itemized list of any charges—like cleaning or repairs—and attach receipts or estimates when possible. Send this to the tenant's forwarding address if they gave you one. If not, send it by certified mail to the last known address, which is usually the rental property. You can also send a copy to their workplace or emergency contact if needed. This is why it's so important to collect complete contact information during the application process; it gives you options if they disappear.

Navigating Ongoing Tenancy Challenges

Even with great screening and solid systems in place, issues will come up. Tenants may pay late, damage property, or break rules. The key is how you respond. Staying calm, consistent, and professional helps protect your peace of mind and keeps your rental business running smoothly. Clear communication, documented policies, and firm boundaries go a long way in resolving problems before they spiral out of control.

Dealing with Chronically Late Rent: Consistency Is Compassion

Early in my management experience, I made the mistake of allowing late rent payments, thinking I was being flexible and understanding.

What I didn't realize was that this approach quickly became a pattern—one that created unnecessary stress, blurred expectations, and weakened the structure of the lease. By trying to be accommodating, I was unintentionally enabling behavior that disrupted both the business and the tenant's accountability.

I've since learned that consistency isn't just about enforcing rules, it's about creating clarity. When you apply the lease terms uniformly, tenants know exactly where they stand. There's no room for confusion, negotiation, or resentment. Clear boundaries and prompt action provide stability for the tenant and peace of mind for the landlord. And while you can't control every tenant's expectations or how they respond to structure, staying consistent protects your peace and keeps your business on solid ground.

Start by enforcing the lease exactly as it's written. If there's a late fee or a grace period, follow it. The lease is your agreement; it's there to protect both sides. As soon as the grace period ends, send a late notice. In my state, if rent still isn't paid, I follow up with a "7-Day Notice to Pay Rent or Quit." This isn't about being harsh; it's about being clear and fair.

Also, keep things professional. Don't let emotions or personal stories cloud your judgment. Stick to the facts and the lease. If you choose to offer a payment plan, put it in writing and make the exception clear that it's not a new standard. This way, you protect the relationship while still running your rental like a business.

When to File for Eviction

Eviction should always be a last resort, but sometimes it's necessary. If all other efforts to resolve the issue have failed, filing for eviction is how you protect your property and keep things moving forward. It's not about punishing the tenant, it's about making sure your rental can serve its purpose.

Make sure you understand your local eviction laws and paperwork ahead of time so you're not scrambling if the situation arises. Also, set aside money in your budget for legal fees or court costs. That way, you're not stuck in a bad situation just because you can't afford to take action.

Managing Maintenance Requests: Responsiveness and Efficiency

Taking care of maintenance issues quickly is one of the best ways to keep tenants happy, protect your property, and stay on the right side of the law. It might seem like a hassle in the moment, but small problems can turn into big ones if ignored.

The first step is to set up a clear system for reporting issues. Let tenants know exactly how to reach you—whether it's by email, phone, or an online portal. For non-emergencies, ask for requests in writing so you have a record and nothing gets missed.

Once you get a request, figure out how urgent it is. Not all repairs are equal. A leaking pipe or broken heater in winter needs immediate attention. A loose cabinet handle can wait a few days. Prioritizing helps you stay on top of emergencies without losing track of routine fixes.

Here's a real example: I once got a call that the HVAC wasn't working. I sent a licensed technician right away, and they said the compressor needed replacing. I approved the repair, but something didn't sit right. I had just replaced that compressor not long ago. Because I had good records, I brought it up, and it turned out the real issue was just a blown fuse. That saved me hundreds of dollars and a lot of frustration. It was a great reminder that keeping notes and asking questions really pays off.

Also, build a solid list of trusted contractors and vendors. Get quotes when you can, approve the work before it starts, and follow up to make sure it's done right. A reliable team makes everything easier.

And don't forget to communicate. Let tenants know what's happening, when someone is scheduled to arrive, if a part is delayed, or when the repair is complete. Keeping them in the loop prevents misunderstandings, reduces frustration, and reinforces that their concerns are being taken seriously.

Handling Difficult Tenants: Grace, Truth, and Firm Action

At some point, you'll encounter tenants who repeatedly violate lease terms, show disregard for the property, or fail to meet their obligations. Managing these situations requires a steady balance of grace, truth, and firm action.

Start by documenting everything. Keep detailed records of phone calls, emails, and in-person interactions. Supplement your notes with photos or videos of any lease violations. This documentation becomes critical if legal action is ever required.

Always anchor your conversations in the lease. It's your framework for expectations and accountability. Referring back to the lease keeps the discussion factual and professional—not personal or emotional.

Know your state's landlord-tenant laws regarding proper notice prior to eviction. In my state, I must issue a formal "7-Day Notice of Noncompliance," commonly known as a 7-business-day pay or quit notice. These notices serve as legal documentation and clearly communicate the seriousness of the issue to the tenant.

Just as important: avoid emotional engagement. Stay calm, firm, and professional. Arguing, raising your voice, or reacting emotionally only weakens your position and can complicate enforcement.

Know when it's time to involve legal counsel. If violations continue or the situation escalates, consult a landlord-tenant attorney. Be financially prepared by setting aside funds for legal action in advance.

Taking these steps isn't punitive; it's responsible stewardship of your property, your business, and your peace of mind.

The Eviction Process: A Necessary Last Resort

Eviction is never easy. It's difficult for everyone involved: the tenant, the landlord, and often even the neighbors. But there are times when it becomes necessary to protect your property, your finances, and your responsibility as a steward.

One of the best pieces of advice I ever received was to attend a few eviction court proceedings before ever needing to file one yourself. Seeing the process firsthand gives you clarity, helps you understand the paperwork, and prepares you for what to expect if and when the time comes.

A few key principles to keep in mind:

Understand Your State's Law: Eviction laws vary widely by state, and sometimes even by county. You must follow every legal step precisely, from notice periods to filing procedures and court appearances. Skipping a step or assuming you know the rules can result in your case being dismissed, costing you time, money, and energy.

Separate Action from Personal Judgment: Eviction is not about punishing someone; it's about enforcing a broken agreement. Your role is to protect your asset and uphold fairness. Enforcing the lease maintains the integrity of your business and ensures other tenants aren't negatively impacted by ongoing violations.

Protecting Your Stewardship Is Not Sin: Allowing repeated violations, whether it's nonpayment, property damage, or disruptive behavior, undermines your ability to manage the property responsibly. Stewardship requires courage and diligence. Holding tenants accountable is part of honoring the responsibility God has entrusted to you.

Be Prepared: Eviction can be time-consuming, expensive, and emotionally draining. Have a plan in place for court appearances, coordinating with the sheriff's office for writs of possession, and handling abandoned belongings in accordance with local law. Set aside funds for these expenses before you ever need them. Being financially prepared helps you avoid delays, resist pressure to compromise, and maintain professionalism throughout the process.

While eviction should always be a last resort, approaching it with knowledge, preparation, and a clear sense of duty allows you to act wisely and uphold both legal and spiritual accountability. It's one of many responsibilities that come with managing property well.

From move-in to move-out, and through every challenge in between, your role as a landlord is about more than collecting rent; it's about stewardship. With diligence, clear communication, and consistent enforcement of fair boundaries, you reduce stress, protect your assets, and honor your calling as a Christian landlord.

And before you move on, one final reminder: document everything. Take notes and timestamp photos, even for issues that seem minor. That dried-out toilet photo you snap today may be the proof you need in court tomorrow.

Chapter 8 Reflections and Takeaways: Managing the Tenancy Lifecycle & Challenges

Key Truths to Carry Forward

- **Thorough documentation protects both landlords and tenants.** Clear, consistent records, from move-in photos to maintenance logs, are your first line of defense against disputes. Documentation isn't about distrust; it's about clarity. It ensures fairness, preserves relationships, and provides legal protection when needed. Just as a shepherd keeps careful watch over his animals, a landlord must know the condition of the property and the history of each tenancy.

- **Full deposits upfront secure commitment.** Handing over keys before receiving the full security deposit is a gamble that rarely ends well. It signals leniency before the lease even begins and can set the tone for future boundary-testing. Require full payment before move-in to establish mutual accountability from day one. This is not about being harsh; it's about honoring the agreement and protecting the stewardship God has entrusted to you.

- **Consistency in enforcement builds stability**. A lease without enforcement is like a house without a foundation; it will eventually crumble. When tenants see that rules are applied fairly and consistently, it builds trust and predictability. Inconsistency, on the other hand, invites confusion, excuses, and resentment. Wisdom means knowing when to show grace and when to stand firm.

- **Having clear systems, trusted vendors, and legal knowledge in place helps you act decisively when challenges arise**. Crisis is not the time to start building your network. Know your eviction process, have a go-to attorney, and build relationships with reliable contractors before you need them. Systems create calm. Preparation prevents panic.

- **Ignoring small repairs lets minor issues grow into costly problems.** That leaky faucet or cracked tile may seem insignificant today, but left unchecked, it can lead to water damage, mold, or tenant frustration. Prompt attention to small issues protects your investment and shows tenants that you care.

Action Steps to Apply

1. Do you have a move-in checklist ready? A thorough move-in process sets the tone for the entire tenancy.

2. Plan for eviction. While you hope never to use it, you must be financially and procedurally prepared to handle serious lease

violations. Know your state's laws, have funds set aside, and understand the steps before you need them.

3. Assess your readiness for challenges. Do you have trusted vendors, legal contacts, and systems in place to handle maintenance, lease violations, or emergencies calmly and professionally?

If you've been thinking, "I need a better system for all of this," you're not alone. Most landlords don't start with everything in place. That's why I've created a separate bundle of customizable templates to support you beyond these chapters—tools like the Tenant Management Policy, Screening Checklist, and Scope of Work Agreement, as well as practical forms for the challenges we've covered here, such as the Move-In/Move-Out Condition Report, General Lease Violation Notice, and 7-Day Pay or Quit Notice.

These are part of a larger set of 23 digital templates I use personally to manage properties with peace, purpose, and alignment. I'll share full details about the complete bundle at the end of the book, so you can explore it when you're ready and choose what best supports your stewardship journey.

Prayer of Strength

Lord, thank You for the trust You have placed in me to steward the properties and responsibilities under my care. Help me to manage them with diligence, fairness, and integrity, reflecting Your grace and justice in every decision. Give me wisdom to act, patience to listen, and courage to enforce what is right. In Jesus's name, Amen.

Scriptures to Meditate On

- **Proverbs 27:23 –** *"Be diligent to know the state of your flocks, and attention to your herds."* Stay attentive to your properties and tenants. Stewardship begins with awareness.

- **Matthew 10:16 –** *"Be wise as serpents and innocent as doves."* When dealing with difficult tenants or enforcing lease terms, wisdom and discernment are essential. This verse reminds us to act with both strategic clarity and spiritual grace—firm, but fair.

- **Ecclesiastes 3:1 –** *"For everything there is a season..."* There will be seasons of peace and seasons of conflict. Wise landlords prepare for both, knowing that structure brings peace even in hard seasons.

- **Colossians 4:6 –** *"Let your speech always be gracious, seasoned with salt, so that you may know how you ought to answer each person."* Whether you're writing a rent reminder or addressing a lease violation, your words matter. Grace doesn't mean avoiding truth—it means delivering it with care, clarity, and respect.

Chapter 9: Cultivating Community: Valuing Your Responsible Tenants

U p to this point, our focus has largely been on establishing robust defenses; conquering internal struggles, setting firm boundaries, meticulously screening tenants, and crafting comprehensive leases. These are indispensable tools for protecting your investment and your peace of mind. However, operating as a Christian landlord means going beyond merely avoiding problems. It means actively fostering an environment of mutual respect and stable relationships. This brings us to a crucial, often overlooked aspect of property management: proactively valuing your responsible tenants.

It's a common reality that even the most diligent and fair landlords may not always receive overt appreciation or acknowledgment from tenants. You may wonder if going the extra mile is truly worth it when gestures aren't consistently reciprocated. But as stewards of God's resources, our actions are not driven solely by recognition. They are grounded in faith, integrity, and the pursuit of peace. Intentionally showing appreciation to responsible, communicative, and respectful tenants isn't just "nice." It is a wise, strategic, and biblically sound approach to cultivating long-term stability, and it yields results that often extend far beyond what you can measure on paper.

The Return on Investment (ROI) of Valuing Good Tenants

Investing in your tenant relationships—especially with those who consistently honor the lease—offers real, tangible benefits that far outweigh any small financial cost or effort. And, let's be honest, at times it sure feels like good tenants are harder to find than good properties.

When tenants feel respected and valued, they are far more likely to renew their lease, drastically reducing vacancy rates, marketing expenses, and the time-consuming process of screening new applicants.

I've seen this play out firsthand. One tenant, Anthony, had been renting from me for two years and consistently took excellent care of the property. He often commented on how responsive I was to maintenance requests—even once bragging to a friend that I had replied while traveling out of town. That kind of attentiveness made him feel respected, and in turn, he respected the home. His lease renewals were effortless, and his presence brought stability to the property. At the end of his tenancy, he referred a friend to the property, sharing how well it had been maintained. That friend went on to become an excellent tenant as well.

Another moment stands out as a reminder that grace and discernment often go hand-in-hand. I once received a call at around 7 a.m. on Christmas morning. The tenant was furious, the oven had stopped working, and she needed it to cook her turkey and other holiday dishes. It had worked the night before and had been reliable for months, but it chose that morning to fail.

I did everything I could to find a repair technician, but unsurprisingly, no one was available—most were celebrating Christmas themselves. Her husband eventually took the phone and said, "Mrs. Armstrong, it's Christmas. I know you can't get someone here this morning. I called my mother, and we can use her oven; we're having dinner there anyway." Meanwhile, his wife could still be heard in the background, cursing and ranting.

By that evening, I had scheduled the appliance repair. And while I wasn't obligated to do anything more, I chose to send them a $50 gift card for the inconvenience. It wasn't about rewarding poor behavior, it was about honoring the situation with grace, and reinforcing that I take tenant comfort seriously, even when circumstances are out of my control.

When tenants feel ownership over their space—even as renters—they tend to take better care of it. They report maintenance issues promptly, prevent damage, and treat the home with pride and responsibility.

Respect also fosters openness. A valued tenant is much more likely to reach out with concerns early, giving you a chance to address issues before they escalate into costly problems. This kind of relationship also makes misunderstandings easier to resolve. Difficult conversations don't feel adversarial when there's a history of fairness and mutual trust.

There is also a ripple effect. Satisfied tenants talk. They may quietly recommend your property to friends or colleagues, which becomes an intangible but powerful asset: your reputation as a fair and respectful landlord. And finally, managing properties where tenants respect your time, your property, and the lease agreement is simply less stressful. It allows you to manage your business without resentment or dread, making your role more sustainable and even joyful.

Biblical Principles for Blessing Others

Your role as a landlord isn't just about properties; it's also about people. Every interaction, every policy, and every decision is an opportunity to reflect the heart of God. Scripture gives us clear, timeless principles for how we're to treat others, even within business.

> *"Give, and it will be given to you. A good measure—pressed down, shaken together, and running over—will be poured into your lap. For with the measure you use, it will be measured to you."* — Luke 6:38

This verse isn't limited to financial generosity. It speaks to the posture of our hearts—how we extend grace, respect, and fairness in ways that mirror God's character. In property management, this might look like responding promptly to maintenance requests, offering clear communication during tense moments, or showing compassion when a tenant faces hardship.

When you lead with generosity not just in money, but in patience, dignity, and integrity, you create an atmosphere where tenants feel safe, valued, and respected. And often, that atmosphere leads to longer tenancies, better property care, and fewer conflicts.

Blessing others doesn't mean compromising your boundaries. It means honoring people while honoring the structure you've built. When you do both, you reflect a kingdom mindset—one that sees every lease, every home, and every tenant as part of a bigger story.

> *"So in everything, do to others what you would have them do to you, for this sums up the Law and the Prophets."* —Matthew 7:12

Being firm in business does not mean being cold. Stewardship includes treating tenants the way we would want to be treated if the roles were reversed. Respect and kindness are not signs of weakness—they are signs of integrity, maturity, and spiritual alignment.

When we apply biblical principles to property management, we begin to see that appreciation and accountability can coexist. You can uphold boundaries and enforce policies while still honoring the humanity of the people you serve.

Practical Ways to Show Appreciation *(Without Compromising Boundaries or Profits)*

Appreciation doesn't require expensive gifts or crossing professional lines. Often, it's the small, thoughtful gestures that speak the loudest.

- **Timely maintenance and repairs.** Simply doing what the lease promises, and doing it promptly, shows care for your tenant's comfort and well-being. It's a quiet but powerful form of respect.

- **Consistent communication** Responding to messages within 24 to 48 hours, even if only to confirm receipt and share a timeline, fosters trust and transparency. Tenants feel seen and heard.

- **One-time gestures of gratitude:** A welcome basket at move-in stocked with basic necessities, a holiday greeting card in December, or a handwritten thank-you note after a smooth lease renewal can make a lasting impression. These gestures say, "I notice you. I value your responsibility."

- **Modest tokens for long-term tenants.** For those with a strong history, a $10–$15 gift card to a local coffee shop or grocery store can be appropriate. Even a one-time late fee waiver—used sparingly, communicated clearly, and reserved for legitimate emergencies—can reinforce trust with responsible tenants.

- **Recognition of longevity and care.** Tenants who consistently renew and maintain the property well deserve acknowledgment. A gift card to a local restaurant, a free carpet cleaning at renewal, or a simple note of thanks can go a long way in reinforcing that their stewardship is noticed and appreciated.

These gestures aren't about being flashy or indulgent; they're about cultivating a culture of mutual respect. When tenants feel valued, they're more likely to stay, care for the property, and contribute to a peaceful rental experience. And when you lead with integrity, you reflect the heart of God—even in the details.

Maintaining Boundaries While Showing Care

Appreciation should never become favoritism or blur professional lines. I've learned this firsthand. For example, I have a habit of answering the phone with, "Hi honey," or even, "Sweetheart, how are you?" While harmless with family and friends, that kind of language isn't wise with tenants or contractors. It communicates a familiarity that can be misinterpreted and unintentionally shifts the dynamic.

Showing care and compassion can still be warm and friendly without crossing into gestures or language that imply a relationship beyond landlord and tenant. Responsible stewardship means staying professional and consistent. Keep gestures modest and infrequent. Always be clear that no gift changes lease obligations. And never accept or exchange gifts in connection with late rent or lease violations.

Appreciation works best when it reinforces responsibility and trust, not when it compromises them. When done well, it strengthens your authority, not undermines it.

The Blessing Flows Both Ways

When you choose to proactively value your good tenants, you're planting seeds of peace, trust, and mutual respect. Over time, these relationships reduce your stress, protect your investment, and cultivate a sense of order and calm in your properties.

You're not just creating a good business, you're living out your role as a faithful steward. Even if you never hear "thank you," tenants often respond with continued care, long-term tenancy, and quiet trust. And if they don't, that doesn't mean your efforts were wasted.

The beauty of God's economy is this: nothing sown in faith is ever lost.

Chapter Summary

Treating responsible tenants with care, consistency, and respect is one of the most overlooked strategies in long-term property management success. It's easy to focus on screening new applicants or resolving conflicts, but sustaining peace often comes from nurturing the relationships that are already working. When tenants feel valued, they tend to stay longer, care for the property, and communicate more openly, saving you time, money, and stress.

This approach isn't just wise and fruitful; it's deeply spiritual. Scripture reminds us that our work reflects our worship. Colossians 3:23 says, *"Whatever you do, work at it with all your heart, as working for the Lord..."* That includes how we respond to maintenance requests, how we communicate during lease renewals, and how we show appreciation without compromising boundaries. Good tenants aren't guaranteed, but when you have them, steward the relationship as faithfully as you steward the roof over their heads. Doing so reflects God's character, protects your peace, and builds a foundation for long-term success.

Chapter 9 Reflections and Key Takeaways: Cultivating Community

Key Truths to Carry Forward

- Respecting responsible tenants reduces turnover, improves communication, and protects your investment.

- Your actions reflect God's grace, integrity, and fairness—even if appreciation isn't overtly returned.

- Small, thoughtful gestures matter.

- Appreciation should never compromise lease enforcement or create favoritism.

- Boundaries and care can coexist.

Action Steps to Apply

1. Consider your tenant relationships. Are you proactively noticing and valuing responsible tenants?

2. Assess your communication. Do your tenants feel heard and respected through timely responses and updates?

3. Schedule a property check. Make sure maintenance is up-to-date to show tenants that their comfort and care matter.

4. Send a gesture of appreciation. A short thank-you note, small gift card, or holiday greeting to a long-term or high-performing tenant.

5. Review boundaries. Make sure all gestures are modest, professional, and tied to behavior/lease performance, not personal preference.

Prayer of Gratitude

Lord, thank You for the gift of good tenants and for the peace they bring to my work as a steward of Your property. Help me to pause and see their value, not just in financial terms, but as people made in Your image. Give me a heart that notices these blessings and responds with gratitude rather than taking them for granted. In Jesus's name, amen.

Scriptures to Meditate On

- **Matthew 7:12** "So in everything, do to others what you would have them do to you, for this sums up the Law and the Prophets." The Golden Rule calls us to treat others as we would want to be treated. In property management, this means honoring not just responsible tenants, but all tenants with timely responses, fair treatment, and clear expectations. It's not about favoritism, it's about integrity.

- **Luke 6:38** "Give, and it will be given to you. A good measure, pressed down, shaken together and running over, will be poured into your lap. For with the measure you use, it will be measured to you.", reminds us that generosity—whether in grace, time, or attention, often returns as a blessing. A simple thank-you note, a modest gift card, or a holiday greeting can reinforce trust and encourage continued care.

- **Romans 12:18** *"If it is possible, as far as it depends on you, live at peace with everyone."* Proactively valuing good tenants is one of the most effective ways to cultivate peace in your properties. It's a form of stewardship that honors both your investment and your calling.

Chapter 10: Protecting Your Well-Being: Sustaining Yourself as a Christian Landlord

L andlording is not just a business; it's an emotional, spiritual, and mental challenge. While this book has focused on systems, leases, and stewardship of tenants and property, you—the landlord—are also a steward of yourself. Without caring for your own well-being, even the best systems won't matter, because you'll be too worn down to carry them out.

This chapter is about preserving yourself. If you don't manage your emotions, energy, and expectations, your properties will end up managing you. And when that happens, it can feel as though nothing else exists except "properties."

It's like being trapped in a house with no windows—every room filled with leases, notices, and maintenance requests. The walls close in, and soon you forget that outside those walls, there is fresh air, family, ministry, and purpose.

Let's pause and acknowledge this truth: landlording is only one aspect of your life. If it has become the only aspect—or if you've allowed it to consume your life—then you don't just need this book. You need to step back and reclaim your life.

God never called you to be swallowed whole by real estate. And let's be honest—people get swallowed whole by all sorts of things: pastoring, entrepreneurship, parenting, caregiving, ministry work, and climbing the career ladder. Anything—even a good thing—can consume you if it becomes the only thing.

Balance, balance, balance is key.

Balance means choosing to turn off your phone at dinner. Balance means letting a maintenance request wait until morning instead of losing sleep. Balance means remembering that your worth is not tied to your rental income or your tenant's behavior.

It doesn't mean neglecting your responsibilities—it means putting them in their proper place. Stewardship is not slavery. Ownership is not an obsession. The goal is not just profit, but peace.

God didn't design you to be devoured by your calling, business, or property. He designed you to live a whole, balanced, and worshipful life.

The Emotional Toll of Property Management

Even with strong systems in place, property management can be draining. There are late payments to chase, emergencies that demand attention, legal notices to issue, angry tenants to calm, entitled attitudes to confront, and the never-ending pressure of finances, repairs, and expectations.

Over time, these stressors can wear down your patience, compassion, and clarity. What began as a wise investment can quickly morph into a constant spiritual and emotional drain. The hidden cost of landlording isn't always financial—it's the slow toll it can take on your mind and soul.

Acknowledge the Weight You Carry

Too often, landlords minimize what they're carrying. But you're not just managing rent checks and leases—you're navigating conflict, enforcing rules, confronting injustice, and sometimes absorbing someone else's crisis. That is real weight.

Scripture reminds us what to do with it:

"Come to me, all you who are weary and burdened, and I will give you rest."

—Matthew 11:28

It's not a weakness to admit the work is hard—it's wisdom. Acknowledgment is the first step toward relief.

Boundaries Are Not Just for Tenants

One of the quickest paths to burnout is enforcing lease boundaries while violating your own. Many landlords do this without realizing it—answering calls at all hours, dropping everything to handle minor issues, internalizing tenant problems, and allowing the business to operate without any margin for rest.

I once had a tenant brag that I responded to their request while I was out of town, as if that proved my excellence as a landlord. At the time, I thought so too. Today, I recognize it was actually proof of poor boundaries. What I thought was professionalism was really self-neglect.

I had to learn that not every tenant's "emergency" is truly an emergency. For example, I once rushed to fix a Friday night toilet issue, thinking that was what a "good landlord" does—only to realize later that the tenant had two bathrooms and the issue could have easily waited until Monday.

Discernment and communication go hand-in-hand. Now, I'm clear in my leases about what qualifies as an emergency and how I handle them. This prevents unnecessary stress and reminds both me and my tenants that I am not on-call for every whim.

To support this boundary, I now have a part-time property manager who is on-call when I'm on vacation or unavailable. This ensures coverage without sacrificing my personal time or peace. Some landlords trade off with one another, covering each other's properties during travel or emergencies. Others rely on management companies that offer temporary on-call support. Whatever the method, the goal is the same: to protect your well-being while maintaining responsible coverage.

Boundaries are not selfish—they're strategic. They allow you to serve well without being consumed. And they remind everyone involved that stewardship includes caring for the steward.

Don't Let a Tenant's Emergency Become Your Identity Crisis

Tenants will sometimes bring drama, manipulation, or guilt, hoping to pressure you into ignoring the lease or financing their crisis. Compassion has its place—but you cannot absorb someone else's irresponsibility as your own. If you do, you will drown under the weight of it.

Remember: you can be kind without being controlled. Boundaries are not a lack of compassion—they are a form of wisdom. You are called to steward your properties, not rescue people from the consequences of their choices.

Build a Support System

This work can feel isolating. Many Christian landlords don't have a community that understands the unique mix of ministry and management that comes with this calling. That's why it's so important to build your own circle of support.

Join a local or online landlord group. Seek out a Christian business or accountability group if you can find one. Meet regularly with a mentor, counselor, or spiritual adviser. Create rhythms of prayer and reflection within your monthly business practices. And don't be afraid to start a group yourself—you may be the very person other landlords in your area are waiting for.

You were never meant to carry this alone.

Accept That You Will Make Mistakes

Even with all the right systems, you will misjudge tenants, delay actions, lose money, get emotionally entangled, or react out of frustration. You will have days when you feel like giving up. That does not make you a failure—it makes you human.

The key is to learn, adjust, and forgive yourself. Scripture reminds us:

"There is now no condemnation for those who are in Christ Jesus."

—Romans 8:1

That includes the moments when you fall short as a landlord. Grace is not just for your tenants—it's for you, too.

Reclaim Your "Why"

When stress builds and decisions weigh heavily, you must return to your "why." Why did you begin this journey? What did you hope it would provide for your family, your faith, and your future? Are you operating out of fear—or out of faith?

This isn't just real estate. It's a calling. But your calling should not crush you—it should anchor you.

Make Time for Rest and Renewal

Rest is not optional. It is a biblical command. If you do not schedule rest, stress will schedule itself—and it will always collect its payment in full.

Rest can take many forms:

- A weekly Sabbath where work is set aside

- A weekend each quarter dedicated to prayer and planning

- An annual retreat with a spouse or accountability partner

- Simply weekends that are truly work-free

Delegating tasks or hiring part-time help is not failure—it is wisdom. Your health, faith, and family are worth more than handling every detail personally.

Measure Success by Peace, Not Just Profit

Profit matters. Cash flow, equity, and appreciation are all important. But success cannot be measured by financial metrics alone. Mental clarity, emotional resilience, and spiritual peace are also part of the balance sheet.

If your properties are producing income but robbing you of joy, something is off.

Scripture is blunt:

"Better a little with the fear of the Lord than great wealth with turmoil."

—Proverbs 15:16

You were not called to be a landlord at the expense of your soul.

Chapter Summary

In this final chapter, we shift the spotlight from properties and tenants to you—the manager, the decision-maker, the steward. No amount of income or success is worth the loss of your health, your peace, or your identity in Christ.

Protect yourself. Honor your limits. Pursue rhythms of rest. And remember: you are not alone.

"He restores my soul. He guides me in paths of righteousness for His name's sake." —Psalm 23:3

Faithful stewardship begins with you.

Chapter 10 Reflections And Key Takeaways: Protecting Your Well-Being—Sustaining Yourself as a Christian Landlord

Key Truths to Carry Forward

- Stewardship includes yourself. Managing property is important, but neglecting your own health and peace will sabotage everything else.

- Boundaries sustain you. Just as leases protect tenants, personal limits protect your mind, spirit, and family.

- Not every problem is your problem. Compassion does not mean carrying crises that aren't yours to bear.

- Support brings strength. You don't have to manage this journey alone—wise counsel, community, and prayer are lifelines.

- Peace is a measure of success. Profit without joy is not God's design. True success is income with inner calm and spiritual renewal.

Action Steps to Apply

1. Audit your boundaries. Write down and adjust where you've allowed tenants' needs to intrude on rest, family, or faith.

2. Schedule intentional rest. Put quarterly retreats, weekly downtime, or Sabbath rhythms into your calendar today.

3. Build your circle. Reach out to one mentor, accountability partner, or group that can encourage you in this work.

4. Revisit your "why." Journal on what drew you into landlording, how it serves your bigger purpose, and whether fear or faith is driving your decisions.

Prayer for Sustainment

Lord, thank You for protecting my mind, body, and soul. Help me to remember that rest and relaxation are not luxuries but a command from You to steward my own temple. Guard my heart from burnout and bitterness, and remind me that true success is found in Your peace, not just profit. Help me set healthy boundaries, lean on wise support, and rest in Your presence. In Jesus's name, amen.

Scriptures to Meditate On

- **Matthew 11:28** *"Come to me, all you who are weary and burdened, and I will give you rest."* Landlord fatigue is real—especially when dealing with difficult tenants, maintenance issues, or financial pressure. This verse reminds you that rest isn't found in perfect tenants or flawless systems, but in Christ. When you feel overwhelmed, pause and invite God into your stewardship. Rest is not the absence of responsibility—it's the presence of peace in the midst of it.

- **Romans 8:1** *"There is now no condemnation for those who are in Christ Jesus."* It's easy to feel guilt over past mistakes—whether you were too lenient, too harsh, or simply didn't know better. But this chapter encourages growth, not shame. It affirms that you can move forward in grace. Responsible stewardship includes learning from missteps without carrying condemnation. You're not defined by what you didn't do— you're empowered by what you're becoming.

- **Proverbs 15:16** *"Better a little with the fear of the Lord than great wealth with turmoil."* This verse speaks directly to the temptation to prioritize profit over peace. Honoring responsible tenants and cultivating community may not always yield the highest financial return—but it produces lasting fruit. A peaceful property with long-term tenants is often more valuable than constant turnover chasing higher rent. Stewardship is about balance, not burnout.

- **Psalm 23:3** *"He restores my soul. He guides me in paths of righteousness for His name's sake."* Managing property can feel like a grind, but this verse offers a spiritual reset. When you choose to treat tenants with care, enforce boundaries with integrity, and lead with consistency, you're walking in righteousness—not just professionalism. Let God restore your soul and guide your decisions. Your work as a landlord is part of your walk with Him.

Conclusion
Faithful Stewardship for the Long Haul

As you reach the end of this journey, take a moment to acknowledge something important: you've done something most landlords never do. You've chosen to approach real estate not simply as a business, but as a ministry of stewardship—rooted in biblical values, sustained by faith, and executed with diligence, clarity, and grace.

You've wrestled with hard truths: about your own patterns, your need for healthy boundaries, and the cost of enabling dysfunction. You've developed systems, policies, and strategies not just to protect your properties, but to preserve your peace and honor God in how you manage what's been entrusted to you.

This book has not been about chasing profit for its own sake. It's about keeping profit in proper order—as a fruit of wise stewardship, not an idol to be pursued at all costs. That distinction is what sets apart the Christian landlord.

You are not just a property owner. You are a caretaker of people's homes. You are not just an investor. You are a builder of peaceful neighborhoods. You are not just a manager. You are a leader, a peacemaker, and at times, a protector.

You've Learned How To...

Confront internal habits that were keeping you in landlord bondage

Create ironclad, clear lease agreements that serve as guardrails—not weapons

Screen applicants with both discernment and due diligence

Protect your properties without sacrificing your peace

Respond to conflict and dysfunction in ways that are both firm and fair

Maintain boundaries while still being a blessing

Build systems and partnerships that prevent burnout and promote consistency

And above all, walk out your role in real estate as a form of faithful service

A Calling, Not a Curse

If you've ever asked, "Why did I even get into this?"—you're not alone. Landlord fatigue is real. But stewardship burnout often happens when we lose sight of what we're really doing and why.

This book is your reminder: you were never meant to carry it all alone. Your strength, your insight, your provision—they all come from the Lord. When you manage your properties God's way, you can sleep well, even in the storm.

Being a landlord is not easy—but done faithfully, it is deeply rewarding. And more than that, it is sustainable when you prioritize clarity, boundaries, order, and wisdom.

The Fruit of Faithful Stewardship

Stewardship done well produces fruit—sometimes visible, sometimes unseen:

- A tenant who quietly renews for five more years because you've made her feel secure

- A neighborhood that improves simply because you maintain your property well

- A family that found peace under your roof during a hard season

- Your own family, who sees you less stressed and more present at home because you've built better systems

- And perhaps most important: your own sense of alignment with the Spirit of God, knowing you've managed well what He's placed in your hands

Your Work Is Not in Vain

The world may never applaud you for managing well. Your tenants may not fully understand how many hard decisions you make behind the scenes. But God sees. God rewards faithfulness. And every act of diligence and obedience matters in His economy.

> *"Whatever you do, work heartily, as for the Lord and not for men... You are serving the Lord Christ."* — Colossians 3:23–24

Final Encouragement: Keep Stewarding, Keep Growing

Keep refining your systems.

Keep learning from your mistakes.

Keep seeking God's wisdom before every tough decision.

There will be seasons where it feels like too much—

But don't forget that you're not building alone.

You are co-laboring with Christ,

and He has called you to this for a purpose.

May your properties bring peace,

your tenants bring ease,

and your efforts bring joy.

May you walk in authority, not anxiety.

And may your journey as a Christian landlord

be marked by order, fruitfulness, and peace—

for years to come.

You were never just managing property.

You were always stewarding purpose.

Now, step into your next season of stewardship.

YOUR NEXT SEASON OF STEWARDSHIP STARTS HERE

You've just completed *Beyond Rent Checks: The Faith-Based Guide to Purposeful Property Management*—a journey into faith filled, purpose-driven property management. Now it's time to activate what you've learned.

To support your next steps, I've created a complete ecosystem built around the Sorting Season™ framework. This bundle:

- 📖 The full Beyond Rent Checks book
- ✚ 23 Plug-and-Play Templates
- 🎓 7-Day Quick Start Guide
- 🔍 10-Week Steward's Reflection Guide

Visit LegacyLightPress.com to get the full bundle.

www.ingramcontent.com/pod-product-compliance
Lightning Source LLC
Chambersburg PA
CBHW070915130626
46555CB00001B/142